Stories THAT Preach

A Collection of True-Story Devotionals

MELINDA ROGERS

WESTBOW
PRESS®
A DIVISION OF THOMAS NELSON
& ZONDERVAN

This book is a work of non-fiction. Unless otherwise noted, the author and the publisher make no explicit guarantees as to the accuracy of the information contained in this book and in some cases, names of people and places have been altered to protect their privacy.

WestBow Press books may be ordered through booksellers or by contacting:

WestBow Press
A Division of Thomas Nelson & Zondervan
1663 Liberty Drive
Bloomington, IN 47403
www.westbowpress.com
844-714-3454

All scripture quotations are taken from the Holy Bible, New Living Translation, Copyright © 1996, 2004, 2015 by Tyndale House Foundation. Used by permission of Tyndale House Publishers, Inc., Carol Stream, Illinois 60188. All rights reserved.

ISBN: 979-8-3850-0941-1 (sc)
ISBN: 979-8-3850-0942-8 (e)

Library of Congress Control Number: 2023919236

Print information available on the last page.

WestBow Press rev. date: 01/15/2024

Sometimes we need to laugh. Sometimes we need to smile.
All the time, we need God and the truth of His word.

CONTENTS

CLOWN PANTS

IT WAS 1968, AND TRUITT, who later became my husband, was very excited. His mom had finally agreed to buy him a pair of jeans. Almost all the kids in the eighth grade wore faded Levi's, and he had been waiting much too long. But when his mom returned from shopping, he looked at the "jeans" in horror. They were blue, they looked like jeans, but they were not cotton. They were polyester!

Still determined to fit in, Truitt remembered the tattered hemline trend. "OK," he thought out loud, "I can cut off the hem and 'fringe' them. That will help!" He trimmed each leg with scissors, put them in the laundry, and *hoped*.

Retrieving them from the dryer, his horror grew to panic levels. Cut polyester doesn't "fringe." It curls, it swells—it grows. It poufs and expands with astounding vigor into fat, puffy, fuzz.

In a word, Truitt had clown pants.

Have you ever had a "clown pants" season? Maybe you have tried to make the best of what life has handed you and it just got worse! And, like Truitt and his jeans, maybe you have no workable solutions to the problems. But God does!

Continue to *cry out to Him* and pray! Did you know that many faithful people of the Bible cried out to God in suffering? The faithful prophet Jeremiah asked God why the wicked were so prosperous. He asked why dishonest people were succeeding. Look up Jeremiah 12 to read the words of a leader among men crying out to his father.

If you are a believer in Jesus Christ, then God is your loving, heavenly father. Come to him with your pain. Come to him with your problems. Wait and see. Sometimes God's bigger plan is revealed. Sometimes we live not in understanding, but in the rest of his promises.

One thing is certain: He cares. No matter what, let's continue to find our *contentment* in Him as we realize that we are not enough, He is, and He has a plan.

"I know how to live on almost nothing or with everything. I have learned the secret of living in every situation, whether it is with a full stomach or empty, with plenty or little. For I can do everything through Christ, who gives me strength" (Philippians 4:12–13, NL).

SENIOR SHOPPING

*D*URING THE FIRST WAVE OF the COVID-19 pandemic, I went to the senior shopping hour at Target. Despite that I put on lipstick *and* even earrings, not one employee questioned my age. *What!* I was fully prepared to whip out my driver's license to prove my senior status because surely they would not believe that I was over sixty-five!

I could hear the dialogue in my head. "Yes, I really am a senior. Well, thanks, I hear that a lot—it must be the vitamins. Ha. You are too kind!"

But no. They let me right in the door without so much as a pause. The door attendant just gave me a big "I'm sorry that you are old" smile, and didn't once glance at my pink lips and trendy earrings. Truth be told, I've been getting senior privileges for quite some time! And although no one wants to be considered elderly, there are some perks. The nice Target employees put my groceries in my cart and even offered to take them to my car.

There are, indeed, a few benefits of getting older! Yet one of the best benefits, by far, is the astounding realization that things don't have to be perfect for us to have joy. (In case you've never noticed, our lives are *never* perfect.) I have plenty of joy even though I do not look too young for senior shopping. I have joy despite a lot of other personal trials, which are much, much more serious. Not happiness. Not giddiness. But joy.

I have the joy that believers can experience comes from hope in Him. Sometimes that joy is buried beneath the painful layers of our own sins or the burdens that life throws our way. Sometimes it is buried beneath anxiety and depression, which can have a countless number of causes. Yet, as believers, if we trust God, it is always present as one of the most beloved and life-giving fruits of the spirit. And since God has unstoppable power and unstoppable love, we *can* trust Him. Let's walk toward Him with open arms and ask for joy. He cares.

> "Give thanks to the LORD, for He is good; His love endures forever" (Psalm 107:1, NLT).

STAMPEDE

I WON'T GO INTO THE DETAILS of how it happened, but one evening, years ago, our family found ourselves trapped inside Fossil Rim Wildlife Park in Granbury, Texas. We had been on the adjoining grounds for a church picnic and were late for the included park visit because of Truitt's deacon duties.

We had entered the back way, viewed a few sites, and then had the eerie, eye-opening realization that no one else was around. We drove a little farther on the twisting road, trying to find our way out. After a long while, we approached the exit. Our hearts sank. The gates were locked. We were trapped inside! To complete the horror of the moment, a loud peal of thunder rumbled across the sky.

But the drama did not end there. The storm created a stampede atmosphere, and we soon had large, wild animals jumping over our car! Truitt said, "Don't worry, kids. Worst-case scenario, we will spend the night in the car and get out tomorrow." Clarke, who was older and understood the gravity of the situation, began to wail. Our preschooler, Emily, had complete trust in her dad and began to clap her hands with joy. I want to have complete trust in my dad, my heavenly Father. God says to us, "Don't worry." I want to clap my hands and trust Him to protect me through the storm and the wild animals, which seem to surround us.

The Bible tells us that as children of God we can call him *Father*. Emily trusted her earthly father, and I am happy to report that we were, eventually, rescued by a park ranger. Let's try our best to trust our heavenly Father who is more powerful than we can ever even imagine.

"For the Father himself loves you dearly because you love me and believe that I came from God" (John 16:27).

SNOW

*I*T SNOWED ON OUR FORTY-FIFTH anniversary. In Texas, we often receive frozen rain or a few teasing flakes that melt before they hit the ground. But on this Sunday, we had dazzling, swirling, bountiful snow. Unfortunately, the snow started its dance across our land shortly after Truitt left for church. I was home with my elderly mom. I planned to attend online church in front of the fireplace. Sounds cozy and wonderful, doesn't it?

Well, it wasn't.

Sadly, I was not focused on my blessings. With razor-sharp intensity, I was focused on the "what ifs." What if Truitt lost control of his SUV on the slick roads? What if I lost my husband on our anniversary? What if? What if? What if?

The worship service began online, and I sang praises to God. Just as Saul regained his sense of peace as David played the harp, I regained my balance. I heard God speak. There were no audible words, of course, but clear thoughts from Him came to my mind.

Look at you, I sensed Him say, *here you are in the wonderful, amazing situation. You can look out the window and see a winter wonderland. You have a beautiful fire. You have the companionship of your mother, and you even have coffee! Yet, you cannot enjoy these gifts. You are too worried about the future and what might happen. Look at yourself, Melinda. You tend to live your life in blindness. You don't see the blessings in front of you because you are fretting about the future. Stop it. Look at me. Look at me!*

When talking to others, I often use the phrase, "Eyes on Christ. Eyes on Christ." Yet that day, I realized my eyes and heart are often anywhere but on Him. I asked for His forgiveness and gave Truitt's drive home and everything about my future to Him.

When Truitt walked in the door, I was relieved to hear that he had not seen my five hundred (well, maybe note *quite* that many) desperate texts asking him to come home. He had stayed focused on his music ministry with the kids and had a great morning with eyes on Him. I have to remember that. Let's keep learning!

> "We do this by keeping our eyes on Jesus, the champion who initiates and perfects our faith" (Hebrews 12:2).

SKIRTS ON FIRE

I ONCE HAD AN ADORABLE SKIRT. It was red with white polka dots. *The perfect skirt*, I thought, *for the annual Fourth of July party!* It *was* perfect. At least for about forty-five minutes into the event.

It was then, as I stood in a sea of families shooting fireworks, that I felt a tap on my shoulder. "Ma'am," a polite person asked me calmly. "Did you know that your skirt is on fire?"

I am happy to report that I remembered to stop, drop, and roll. My skirt was ruined by a spark from the fireworks buzzing all around me, but my body remained unscathed. A kind person had seen something about me that I had not. He had opened my eyes to a danger I did not see.

I think about that story a lot when I think of community. As we often hear from church leaders, we need others to help us keep walking the safe path toward Jesus. Sometimes we walk around with our skirts on fire, and we don't even know it! We need others to help us *stop* thinking falsely, *drop* the blinders, and *roll* away from those circumstances that are tripping us up. We also simply need friends to laugh and talk with. We need each other.

Sometimes finding community is easy. Sometimes it is hard. Relationships are made up of the good, the bad, and the ugly. But community is vital and well worth the innate difficulties. Let's refuse to hide and slink into our holes. Let's go to church. Let's find community. We can help others as they help us. You need others, and they need you!

> "And let us not neglect our meeting together, as some people do, but encourage one another, especially now that the day of his return is drawing near" (Hebrews 10:25).

MAIL

My friend Donna is the most detail-minded and organized person I know. When my birthday draws near, I know that I can expect the perfect card that is addressed with the perfect retired-teacher handwriting that will arrive exactly one day before my birthday. That's not all: the card will have the perfect festive stamp and an adorable return address label.

Then there is me. Sometime in the fall, it will dawn on me that Donna has a birthday. And even though I have placed her birthday date in my calendar, I may or may not notice it. When I do realize that Donna does, indeed, have a birthday, it will be one day before the day. If by some miracle I remember to pick up a card, I will realize, only after arriving home, that I do not have a stamp. Out of desperation, I will rifle through old mail looking for an un-cancelled stamp that I can peel off and reglue. The next step is to spend ten minutes trying to decide if reusing a stamp is, indeed, ethical since I did pay for and then immediately loose, a pack of stamps last summer.

After the stamp dilemma is resolved, I will begin the great pen search. Oh, yes, I buy lots of pens. I put them in my purse, on my desk, and in the kitchen. But, when push comes to shove and I really need a pen, they either seem to have scattered to the four winds, or are barely pushing out ink.

I appreciate Donna's orderly life more than you can imagine. I am encouraged by her great example to be a better planner. She kindly tells me that she appreciates the way that I care about her and her family. She encourages me, and I encourage her.

God made each of us so very different. We each have our strengths, and we each have our weaknesses. We are happiest when we avoid comparison and can rejoice in other's strengths. We see each other's weaknesses and realize that we just might have a few as well.

> "A spiritual gift is given to each of us so we can help each other" (1 Corinthians 12:7).

SO FINE

WHEN I WAS TEN YEARS old, I sat in the kitchen with my aunt and my mother. I loved listening to their stories, their very definite opinions, and their viewpoints on the ups and downs of life. As I sat there, the topics of discussion switched quickly and landed for a minute on the various types of hair.

"Melinda's hair is extremely fine," my mother said.

"Yes," my aunt agreed. "She has some of the finest hair that I have ever seen." Picture ten-year-old me feeling excited about having such fine and marvelous hair. I had no idea!

The excitement didn't last. "When we say fine, Melinda," my aunt advised, "We don't mean fine as in good. We mean fine as in texture. Each hair on your head is very thin." Oh.

Isn't that just like life? So very often, we think that things are fine and then realize that things are quite different than we assumed. Life is just full of surprises. Some surprises are amazing and good. Some surprises make us want to pull the blankets over our heads and never get out of bed. One of my best friends loves to remind me that nothing surprises God. She is correct! He knows what life holds for us. He knows the good and He knows the bad. There is comfort in that. And we know that He holds us up and holds us together.

Even in the worst of times, we can find the "fine" in what God has allowed in our lives if we stay in His word and in prayer. Let's rest in His loving arms and *trust* Him to provide.

> "When the earth quakes and its people live in turmoil, I am the one who keeps its foundations firm" (Psalm 75:3).

ASSUMPTIONS

*W*HEN WE BUILT OUR HOUSE twenty-five years ago, we wanted aged wood for our floors. We found some great vintage flooring at a scrap yard and fell in love with it. When the owner told us that the wood was salvaged from an old Fort Worth restaurant, my romantic imagination went into overload. I pictured the wood coming from a beautiful turn-of-the-century restaurant patronized by genteel ladies and gentlemen of a bygone era.

I felt very proud of this beautiful flooring as we carefully stacked it on our property. Then I saw some graffiti on one of the planks and burst out laughing. The graffiti said, "I-HOP stinks!"

Our beautiful vintage wood had come from an IHOP, probably circa 1985. I had given a lot of value to a false assumption. I do that in my everyday life as well. I assume that I must do something applause worthy to have value. I assume my schedule must be full to have value. The list goes on. I assume a lot of things about what matters. Sometimes I find it necessary to ponder my assumptions and spend time with God, evaluating how I can really serve Him best. What really matters in life?

Lifting up our built-in assumptions to God can give us a new and wonderful perspective. Ezekiel 36:26 says, "And I will give you a new heart, and a new spirit I will put within you."

> **"And I will give you a new heart, and I will put a new spirit in you. I will take** out your stony, stubborn heart and give you a tender, responsive heart" (Ezekiel 36:26).

CRAB SKIN

SEVERAL YEARS AGO, TRUITT AND I and two very sad grandkids stood solemnly around the grave of Yoda the hermit crab. Just thirty minutes earlier, the kids had arrived to spend the night, and everyone was eagerly anticipating a night of fun and laughter. As soon as our grandson Huston was in the door, he darted excitedly to our crab-a-tat to check on his beloved pets. Then, in an instant, as so often happens, everything changed. Our hearts dropped as we heard a horrible wail. "Yoda is dead!" Huston lamented. "I picked up his shell and he fell right out."

After much hugging and consoling, we scooped up the lifeless form, took him to the backyard, and held a touching crab funeral. We sang a few hymns, and Arden decorated the crab grave with an artful display of sticks and grass.

After the sad event, I went back into the house to remove Yoda's shell from the cage. As I reached into the crab-a-tat, I couldn't believe my eyes! Staring back at me from the shell were the brightest, most fully vibrant hermit crab eyes that I had ever seen. The beloved Yoda was alive and well!

After some quick research, we realized that Yoda had molted. We couldn't stop laughing when we realized that we had just held a funeral for a bunch of crab skin!

Sadly, I sometimes repeat that behavior in my daily living. I mourn for current events in my life or in the world because I don't know the whole story. I forget that God *does*. In fact, He is the *author*! As believers, we don't know what the middles of our stories hold for us, but we know for certain that our stories end well. We know that God wins!

We also know that Christ walks with us wherever we go. "The Lord himself will fight for you. Just stay calm." Exodus 14:14. Don't mourn without hope; trust the author. No more crying over crab skin!

"And I am certain that God, who began the good work within you, will continue his work until it is finally finished on the day when Christ Jesus returns" (Philippians 1:6).

HIBBER SCHOOL

OCCASIONALLY I THINK OF THE students of Hibber School in Addis, Ethiopia, and when I recall their happy faces, I cannot help but smile. I was there years ago on a mission trip, and I've never forgotten those children.

Their school was dilapidated. The restrooms had not worked for years, and the classrooms looked as if they had never seen a janitor's broom. The children's appearances were not much better. They arrived in school uniforms that were tattered and full of holes—yet, they arrived! They came each morning from the dumps where they lived with their mothers in shacks made of garbage. Their mothers gathered trash to sell so that their children could eat. Few of the kids knew their fathers.

These children came to school each day with giant smiles and with *hope*. They knew that if they got an education, they had a chance to leave the dump when they were adults.

Our job at Hibber was to teach a simple language lesson to a group of ten- to thirteen-year-old students by having them write a thank-you card in English. As is shockingly common at Hibber, the teacher never arrived. But the kids were not discouraged. They were eager to learn. At the end of class, they stood up to read their cards, and I was stunned. These kids who had *nothing*, stood up and read the thank-you notes they had written to their teachers and to their mothers. "Thank you for giving birth to me." "Thank you for teaching me."

As they read their notes of gratitude, tears of thankfulness flowed down their faces. Unbelievable. I had never seen anything like this preteen display of raw emotion and thanksgiving. The kids of Hibber School did not hold back. And as they shared, they ended up teaching me. I learned that day that *hope* and gratitude are an amazing and powerful combination. When mixed in equal measure, hope and gratitude can be a mighty spiritual and emotional fuel to propel us forward. Let's have hope and gratitude as we trust God with the problems that confront us every day.

"Be thankful in all circumstances, for this is God's will for you who belong to Christ Jesus" (1 Thessalonians 5:18).

MELINDA ROGERS

MARCH 25, 2002

*T*HAT IS THE DAY THAT my friend Eileen will never forget. That is the day that her life turned upside down. Her husband, Bill, an active father, husband, and corporate recruiter, suffered a debilitating stroke.

Suddenly, Eileen was Bill's caregiver, the only breadwinner, the only able parent, and the case manager for all the endless medical and insurance paperwork. She maintained all these roles until Bill went to be with the Lord almost seventeen years later. Eileen never faltered in her faith. Nehemiah 8:10 says, "The joy of the Lord is your strength." I can easily say that the joy of the Lord was and is Eileen's strength. She, Bill, Truitt, and I laughed together often. As believers, we can trust God and can have light hearts in dark times.

Drink in what my precious friend once wrote about her ability to maintain peace and joy through trials.

> Stress can steal our joy and allow anxiety to replace our peace … When I think about managing stress I look back at others that have travelled through stressful situations and as I read the scripture and look at the book of Exodus, and the Israelites … they experienced plagues and slavery … They struggled as they wandered the wilderness for 40 years … talk about stress … what did they do?? How did they handle stress?? They built altars … altars to The Lord … they recounted their past … Repeatedly building an altar to The Lord.
>
> As a way to remember the ways God had intervened and rescued them … So they could trust God for the future … Remembering is an act of thanksgiving … It is turning your heart over time's shoulder to see all the ways and times God's arms have carried you …
>
> It is developing gratitude for God's provision … And gratitude is a memory of The heart … Our thankfulness shapes our theology … into one of trusting.

I want to be like Eileen.

> "Oh, the joys of those who trust in the Lord, who have no confidence in the proud or in those who worship idols" (Psalm 40:4).

NEXT FIVE MINUTES

WHEN SHE WAS A YOUNG mom with children who were three and five, our much-loved daughter-in-law, Jennifer, was diagnosed with breast cancer. It was a scary and painful time. Jennifer had more strength and determination than I could fathom, but many days, I sat in my office in a state of stunned disbelief. I tried my best to work, but sometimes it seemed impossible. Worry, doubt, fear, pain, helplessness—all these feelings surrounded and dogged me night and day.

There were many friends who served as our anchors during those difficult days, and each helped us through that dark journey in different ways. One of the anchors in the storm was a faithful children's ministry volunteer named Mimi. Because she is hearing impaired, Mimi did not serve directly with the kids on Sundays. Instead, she showed up at church faithfully each Wednesday to do battle with the dreaded color copier. I personally had to fight the desire to post my victory on social media and scream from the rafters with joy if I managed to print one color copy. Mimi, however, always managed to print stacks and stacks of materials for the kids and did so with a smile on her face.

As a breast cancer survivor, Mimi knew just the type of note to send Jennifer after her scary diagnosis. The advice she gave was wise and, for me, life-changing. Mimi encouraged my beautiful daughter-in-law to keep her mind off the future and to be grateful for the present. She suggested that Jennifer keep her mind on the next five minutes. Pause. Look around. She encouraged her to keep a grateful attitude and to fully enjoy each moment. I've thought a lot about the over the past years. Enjoy each moment and thank God.

F. B. Meyer wrote, "This is the blessed life—not anxious to see far in front, or eager to choose the path, but quietly following behind the Shepherd, one step at a time."

> "So don't worry about tomorrow, for tomorrow will bring
> its own worries. Today's trouble is enough for today"
> (Matthew 6:34).

MY DOG!

O NCE, WHEN TRUITT WAS SMALL, he frantically ran to his mother. She was alarmed by his loud sobs and the river of tears flowing down his little boy cheeks.

"What's the matter, Truitt?" she cried.

"My dog got run over," he wailed pathetically.

"Truitt," she said with surprise, "you don't have a dog!"

"Oh."

Like many creative people, Truitt has a great imagination. He had imagined a beautiful dog and then imagined that it was hit by a car! To this day, Truitt still tends to imagine the worst-case scenario. I often remind him, "Truitt, you don't have a dog." And we laugh.

I also tend to fear the worst. Perhaps we all do on some level.

Do you ever lie in bed in the middle of the night pondering the *best*-case scenario? Probably not, but we should. There is no doubt that God is always with us, and He has the *best*-case scenario in store. Of course, also without a doubt, we don't understand His timing or the events He allows, but He does. He knows. He is good! Let's work on imagining the best, because He is the best, and He loves us.

Sometimes, when I am struggling with trusting God, I tell Him that I am simply going to dwell in His love. I make a determined choice to live there and ask God's help to do so. The enemy loves to use our minds for his purposes, but God wants to give our thoughts to Him.

> "And now, dear brothers and sisters, one final thing. Fix your thoughts on what is true, and honorable, and right, and pure, and lovely, and admirable. Think about things that are excellent and worthy of praise" (Philippians 4:8).

PAINT

*I*T WAS 1978, AND WE had just purchased our first home. It was an old house in the neighborhood we had dreamed about. It was a fixer-upper, and back then, we had lots of fixer-upper energy. So, it was great, until …

One day, I spilt a can of paint. Yes, a whole can of thick white paint rushed out in all its oozing glory onto our brand-new powder-blue carpet. I understand that, right now, you might not be able to get past the fact that we had powder-blue carpet. But, believe me, in 1978, powder blue was far out, baby!

So, we had an indoor puddle of gooey paint. What to do? I will be forever grateful for Truitt's wise decision.

"Let it dry," he said. "Then, I'll bet, we can peel it up." He was right! We let it dry for a few days and were able to peel it right off our lovely carpet.

Even now, these many years later, I think of that paint when I have to wait on something. I've waited on resolutions to problems, waited on healing, and waited on provision. Many times, I have been driving down the road and called out to God. Loudly. "Where are you? Help me."

Often, I want the phone to ring with good news. When things don't happen quickly, I want to rush in and try to fix things on my own. But I can hear that small, yet powerful voice whispering to my heart, "Be still and wait."

God knows what He is doing. He has a plan. As we learn to trust Him, waiting can be good.

> "But those who wait on the Lord will find new strength. They will fly high on wings like eagles. They will run and not grow weary. They will walk and not faint" (Isaiah 40:31).

CAN'T COMPARE

I ONCE READ THAT OUR STRONGEST memories are those that involve strong emotions. I guess that I had intense emotions when I heard a pastor speak from our thirteen-inch television years ago, because I've never forgotten his words. Until that point, I was distractedly listening to his talk when he said something very simple. It was something that should be clearly obvious to all believers, yet I had been allowing myself to drown in self-pity over my own minor struggles.

He said, "No matter what you are suffering, your suffering can in no way compare with the suffering of Jesus. We often say that life is unfair, but believe me, there is nothing that compares to our perfect Jesus, who was without *any* sin, yet He died on the cross for our sins." Truthfully, I don't remember his exact words, but that was the gist of his message.

I've gone back to that teaching over and over in my life when those nagging germs of discontent enter my thoughts. When I begin to feel sorry for myself, I remember those words and they become like a medicine to my spirit. Nothing, absolutely nothing I endure compares with the unfair suffering of Christ on the cross. He was humiliated. He was tortured. He died. He did it for us and He was without any sin!

When you think about it, we can never say, "That's not fair!" No earthly unfairness can compare to that unfairness that Jesus endured for us. Thank you, Jesus!

> **"For you know that God paid a ransom to save you from the empty life you inherited from your ancestors. And it was not paid with mere gold or silver, which lose their value. It was the precious blood of Christ, the sinless,** spotless Lamb of God. God chose him as your ransom long before the world began, but now in these last days he has been revealed for your sake" (1 Peter 1:18).

STORM

ONE DAY, WHEN I WAS in the second grade, a giant storm moved over our school. The clouds sucked up all the light, and the afternoon became as black as night. Before long, we could hear the terrifying sound of hailstones pounding relentlessly against our classroom windows. Our teacher moved us into hallway, where we huddled in a quivering row with our hands on our heads. Suddenly, we heard a great shattering sound as the hailstones invaded the classroom, spreading shards of glass in their wake.

And just like that, everything I had learned in Sunday school came into focus. I remembered that God loved me and that I could call on Him at any time. Soon, I was nudging my friends and saying, "Pass it down, *pray!*" After a while, the clouds moved back, and the sun shone through. No one was injured. I truly believe that the storm that hit our school that year woke up something inside of me. Everything I had learned about God suddenly seemed real. The next year, I heard the gospel and accepted Christ.

As we travel through life, we encounter many different types of storms. The difficulties we encounter shake us up and wake us up. We don't like them. We sometimes tremble in their wake. But they send us to Jesus, and that's a great place to be. Let's rest there.

> **"Jesus was in the stern, sleeping on a cushion. The disciples woke him and said to him, "Teacher, don't you care if we drown?"** He got up, rebuked the wind, and said to the waves, 'Quiet! Be still!' Then the wind died down and it was completely calm" (Mark 4:38–39).

NOISE

My friend Lynn and I sat in a restaurant enjoying the last gooey bits of our dessert crepes when she asked me a question. "What is the most difficult part of having your mom live with you?" I knew the answer immediately but was embarrassed to share the truth.

Dealing with Mom's memory loss was difficult. Helping her shower and encouraging her to do her chair exercises was challenging. But those things were not the most difficult. Not at all.

Staring into my friend's caring and earnest face, I decided to tell her the truth. "It's the noise." She nodded and I went on. "I did not realize that sometimes people with dementia make constant noises as a means of comfort. My mom makes a moaning, panting sound almost all day long. I can hear it even when I am upstairs, and she is in the living room. Truthfully, it drives me nuts!"

"Oh my!" Lynn shook her head. "That's terrible. That would drive me nuts too!"

Relief! There was beautiful relief as I poured out my heart to Lynn. She knew that I was irritated (to the max) by a behavior that was out of my mother's control. She understood.

"Well," Lynn said, "I'm just going to pray that you have some heavenly earplugs!" And, you know what? I developed some of those earplugs. I learned, by God's grace, to keep my mind on other things instead of dwelling on the noise. I also learned a few practical tricks like flipping on the bathroom fans to drown out the sound.

I shared my frustrations with a friend. She prayed. Things improved. Honest sharing and loving prayers are the heart of good Christian friendships. God made us for community!

> "Two people are better off than one, for they can help each other succeed. If one person falls, the other can reach out and help. But someone who falls alone is in real trouble" (Ephesians 4:9–10).

MELINDA ROGERS

BLIND

"**H**OW DO YOU LIKE THE flower?" I asked teenaged Clarke as he sat at the breakfast table many years ago.

"What flower?" he asked.

"Clarke! The amaryllis that opened last night. The one that is literally two inches from your nose right now."

"Oh. I like it."

I teased Clarke a lot about that, but I shouldn't have. I learned later that I, also, am sometimes very blind in ways that matter a lot more than an inability to notice a flower. Just ask our daughter.

When Emily was a young woman, she moved to Nashville and took a job as a nanny. She tried to tell me that things just weren't right. The father in the household was always demanding and wanted her by his side. I never really heard her. When my friend Kathy and I visited Emily one week, the difficulty of Emily's situation became painfully obvious. "We're moving her out tonight!" Kathy said. And we did. While the family slept, we crept into Emily's rooms and moved out all her belongings. We rang the doorbell the next morning and told her former boss that she was leaving.

I look back now and wonder at my inability to see the difficulty of Emily's situation. I am grateful for God's protection and for the things He taught us through this experience.

I learned just how blind I could be to the truth that stares me in the face. From that day forward, I have prayed regularly that God will reveal my blind spots to me. He continues to do so, and I am grateful. Let's pray for open eyes and for eyes that can see! Sight and insight are vital!

"How can I know all the sins lurking in my heart?
Cleanse me from these hidden faults" (Psalm 19:12).

MOVING STOP SIGN

EVERAL YEARS AGO, I FAILED to see one of those transportable stop signs that had been rolled out into the middle of a department store parking lot. It was dark and, sadly, I plowed right into it. The next day, I called the insurance company to file a claim. When asked what happened, I said, "I didn't see one of those moving stop signs." The claims adjuster burst out laughing and wouldn't stop!

I'm not sure she ever understood what I meant. The next time I called, she told me that my description of what happened had given her whole team a good laugh at their staff meeting. Oh well! Sometimes we just do not communicate well!

One great thing about prayer is that God understands all our communications, even it if doesn't make sense to others. God knows everything in our hearts and souls when we speak to Him. Even if our words are not perfect, we can never fail to communicate. Never, ever worry about how you communicate with God. Just do it! Pray anytime, anywhere, any way that you can! Praying is vital!

In Philippians 4:6, Paul commands us to run like the dickens from anxiety and run with open arms toward prayer. Let's run with open arms to God, even when we don't feel like it. When he is upset, my husband will often start his prayers with, "God, I don't feel like talking to you right now, but …" I love that. Truitt is honest with God, and honestly pours out his heart. God hears and He cares.

God is your father. He wants to hear from *you*!

> Psalm 116:17 says, "I will sacrifice a thank offering to you and call on the name of the Lord."

YOU GOTTA LAUGH

NEVER, EVER, SAY OK TO overseeing a kids' treasure hunt that involves clues written on a bazillion puzzle pieces. Why, you ask? Well, years ago, I left my church office after a long day and went to verify that the treasure hunt items were in place for the next day's exciting "kids' kamp" activity. I don't recall the details, but the clues were supposed to be written on a puzzle. Each small group was to receive their pieces in a Ziploc bag so that they could assemble them into a puzzle that revealed their clues.

Yet somehow, the volunteer assembly team had misunderstood the directions, and the puzzles were all mixed up. Somehow, I thought I could figure things out myself and put them back together, but my plan did not work.

So, at around nine o'clock that night, I stood in one of the upstairs classrooms with Truitt and my friend/boss, Kathy. On the floor in front of us were literally thousands of puzzle pieces that we had to assemble into puzzles with the correct clues and place them into the bags.

You know what we did? We laughed and laughed! We laughed at the ludicrous situation. We laughed at the late hour and the seemingly impossible task ahead of us. Around midnight, with tears of laughter still streaming down our faces, we finished the task. Laughter got us through it.

I believe that God has given us the gift of laughter for a reason. Proverbs 17:22 says, "A joyful heart is good medicine, but a crushed spirit dries up the bones." So, don't forget to laugh during days of question marks, anxiety, exhaustion, and even stress. Watch a funny movie. Read a funny book. Recall some of the funniest moments in your life and talk about them with your family or friends. Let's keep on looking up and praying. Let's pray for *joy* and laugh out loud!

"All the days of the afflicted are evil but the cheerful of heart has a continual feast" (Proverbs 15:5).

DIAPER PIN

*W*HEN CLARKE WAS A FEW weeks old, I took him in for his first round of shots. "He may be a little uncomfortable," the doctor told me, "so stop by and purchase some baby Tylenol."

When I was at the drug store, Clarke began to scream and wail. He sounded like he was being tortured. "Boy," I thought, "He is having a *bad* reaction to those shots!" My natural reaction was to pat and bounce him as I hurriedly paid for the Tylenol. Yet, strangely, the more I patted him, the louder he screamed.

When I got home, I put Clarke in his bed to change his diaper. To my horror, I noticed that a diaper pin had come undone and was stabbing him in the thigh. His screams weren't a reaction to the shots; they were a reaction to being poked over and over with a big pin that was pushed further into his skin with every well-intentioned pat! I still shutter when I think about that, and Clarke is now a grown man with kids of his own!

Sometimes our natural reactions aren't for the best. When we are bored or frustrated or tired, we can easily turn to television, social media, food, video games, and so on. It's natural to turn to things that console us. And these things, in moderation, are fantastic! But if we binge them or use them as a substitution for time with the Lord, they start jabbing us like a big pin.

How do I know these things? You guessed it! Personal experience. Times of stress often bring temptation to binge on the things that don't bring real comfort. As a matter of discipline, turn to the Bible and time with God instead. Even if you are doing it with a lack of enthusiasm, believe me, you will end up refreshed.

> "Seek the Kingdom of God above all else, and live righteously, and He will give you everything you need" (Matthew 6:33).

MELINDA ROGERS

CHANGES

A FTER TRUITT AND I WERE engaged, we would often run into people who knew him as a child. More than once, these folks from Truitt's early days would shake their heads and say, "I hope and pray that your kids don't turn out like Truitt."

Little wonder. Below is just a partial list of the wild things that he did as a child:

1. Snuck into a mail truck and messed up all the mail.
2. Threw gravel on his neighbor's freshly painted garage door.
3. Stopped the ice cream man with the promise of returning with money, only to watch him out the front window just to see how long he would wait.

To sum it up, when Truitt was a child, things looked *grim*! Yet, God changed all of that when he accepted Christ in the eighth grade. To this day, he still has that mischievous twinkle in his eye and a great sense of fun, but he is a man who loves and serves the Lord.

Christ changes us if we let Him. Often, when we want to make positive changes in our lives to honor God, the enemy whispers lies to us. "You are a loser. You will never change. Give up." When this happens, just tell him to go away and then cry out to Jesus.

With Christ, all things are possible. He makes pathways for us through the wilderness. Let's rely on his strength and his truth.

> "For I am about to do something new. See, I have already begun! Do you not see it? I will make a pathway through the wilderness. I will create rivers in the dry wasteland" (Isaiah 43:19).

ANGEL

I DON'T KNOW IF HE WAS an angel, but he suddenly appeared. I was walking with my parents across the hospital parking lot toward our car. We were too upset to speak. My eighteen-month-old nephew, Kevin, was in a coma in the ICU with a severe head injury.

The doctors weren't sure that he would survive the night. They gave very grave predictions about his life if he did survive. "He may not see. He may not walk. He may not hear ..."

My head was bowed toward the ground when I suddenly saw a fourth set of feet walking beside us. I looked up into a face so full of compassion that I could barely take it in.

"What is the matter?" this fourth person asked us. I told him our story, and he said he would pray for Kevin. Then suddenly, a car came by and whisked him away.

My heart leaped up. I knew something special had happened.

When I got home, I reached for my Bible and it opened to Luke 7:22. I read these astounding words: "The blind receive their sight, the lame walk, lepers are cleansed, and the deaf hear, the dead are raised up ..."

Kevin survived. He walks, talks, sees, and hears. Our God is powerful. He sends help, sometimes in ways we can see and sometimes in ways that we cannot. But He is there. He is good, and He is big.

> "At that very time, Jesus cured many people of their diseases, illnesses, and evil spirits, and he restored sight to many who were blind. Then he told John's disciples, 'Go back to John and tell him what you have seen and heard—the blind see, the lame walk, those with leprosy are cured, the deaf hear, the dead are raised to life, and the Good News is being preached to the poor.' And he added, 'God blesses those who do not fall away because of me'" (Luke 7:21–23).

MUD WALK

ONE DAY WHEN EMILY WAS in college, she got up, got dressed, and decided to take her roommate's big dog for a walk. She had only gotten a few steps when a fellow dog walker came by. Her roommate's dog chased after the other dogs with such ferocity that he managed to pull Emily down and through several large mud puddles before she even knew what hit her.

Have you ever had random thoughts that pop up like a crazed dog trying to pull you through the mud? I have! Sometimes before we even have time to understand what's going on, we start believing lies. It seems to me that there are three ways that this can happen.

- We *create* falsehoods. "I won't get that job. I probably flubbed the interview."
- We *assume* falsehoods. "I haven't called Mary. I'm sure that she's mad at me. I won't bother calling her now."
- We *listen* to falsehoods. "The world is falling apart and there is no hope." Thank you, news media!

Creating, assuming, and listening to lies *is easy*. But the good news is this: When we begin to buy into lies, God can show us the truth.

Sometimes I feel like I am just not right in my spirit. I go to God and say, "God, straighten me out." He does. He brings truth into the places where I have believed lies. I am always weak and susceptible, so I have to go to Him often. Thankfully, He never gives up on us. Watch out for the lies and remember that 2 Corinthians 10:5b says, "Take every thought captive to obey Christ."

**"If you need wisdom, ask our generous God, and he will give it to you. He will not rebuke you for asking"
(James 1:5).**

POWER LINES

ONE DAY I SAT WITH my friend Karen at the local Dairy Queen. We ate our salads, discussed our struggles, and lamented the current state of the country. She was just starting to tell me about the difficult decisions she must make about her upcoming surgery when, out the windows, I could see something alarming.

"Karen," I interrupted her, "I hate to tell you this, but power lines are falling everywhere, and one just hit your car!"

Restaurant staff and customers ran to the windows to see panicked construction workers waving and shouting.

Calling on my vast, spiritual wisdom and insight in times of crisis, I froze into a speechless human statue with my mouth gaping open. As it turns out, those sparking, scary power lines didn't cause any damage, and no one was hurt. But what a strange feeling it was to watch those waving, spinning, wires of fire descending all around us.

There are times when events in our lives surround us like those falling power lines. We live with sparks of fear and don't know what to expect next. One day things are fine, and the next day life is upside down. When those things occur, we can be sure of one thing: we have a line to the greatest power in the universe. He hears us when we call.

No scary thing in your life is greater than the source of all power. God is all love. God is all power. Our Father is incredible. Run into His arms.

> "Jesus looked at them intently and said, 'Humanly speaking, it is impossible. But with God everything is possible'" (Matthew 19:26).

LAMBO

ONE DAY MANY YEARS AGO, Lambo, the puppet, and I made a memorable debut on Easter Sunday. We were a big hit with the preschoolers. In fact, we were such a big hit, that Lambo and I never showed our faces together again! *It was bad.* You might say that our excellence faded as the morning moved on. Other children's staff members, who, by the way, still laugh about this, told me that I started strong. But as the morning progressed and group after group of squirming preschoolers came into the room for their Easter lesson from Lambo, my arms began to droop, and Lambo's cute lamb voice became more and more like my own. Lambo never lost his stitched-on smile, but mine, evidently, was another story. It seems as if Lambo and I had lost heart. My plan to entertain preschoolers for several hours in row was a bad one!

Do you ever feel like you've lost heart? I certainly do. I particularly lose heart when I don't understand the plan that God seems to be unveiling in my life. When I feel that vacancy of enthusiasm in my spirit, I sometimes listen to scriptures set to music. One of my favorites is Seeds' version of "Take heart, take heart, I have overcome the world!" from John 16:33. We must focus on the overcomer of the world. We must focus on the one who renews our strength and who knows the plan.

I once thought about godly focus as I sat on my back porch watching the summer rain. Suddenly, the ceiling on the porch began to leak and I lost my focus on the beauty of God's nourishing rainfall. I focused only on the leak. "Help me, God," I prayed, "to trust you and remember your goodness in providing the water we need for the earth and not focus on the expensive roof repair. You know the plan."

Have I learned the focus lesson to perfection? No. Will I keep working to keep my focus on Him? Yes. Will I ask for the help of the Holy Spirit to do this? Yes! Take Heart! Take Heart! He has overcome the world!

"But those who trust in the Lord will find new strength.
They will soar high on wings like eagles" (Isaiah 40:31a).

WEDDINGS.

*I*N THE SUMMER OF 2008, I found myself in a rented car driving the streets of Smithfield, Virginia. I was looking for the bed and breakfast that we had booked for Emily's wedding reception. Destination weddings are fun but doing all the planning by phone and email is difficult. I had traveled ahead of the rest of the family so that I could take care of all the event preliminaries. My first goal was to check in with the reception venue. As I drove, I became more and more mystified. I was on the right street and the right block, but I could *not* find the beautiful home pictured on the B&B website.

After several trips up and down the same street, something disturbing occurred to me. Could it be? Yes. The structure that was completely covered with and hidden by scaffolding was, you guessed it, the "beautiful" bed and breakfast! The entire exterior was being redone.

As it turns out, the wedding was *not* ruined by the surprise scaffolding. In fact, we captured some funny pics of Emily and Christopher in their wedding attire with tools and paintbrushes in front of all the construction.

If you survey married couples, you will find that it seems almost *every* wedding has an unexpected occurrence. (Ask me sometime about the musician at our wedding who showed up in dirty pants and a tie made from underwear.) Maybe God allows so many unexpected events at weddings to prepare couples for life! Life is full of the unexpected. Some surprises are amazing, and some knock us to the ground. But through all the unexpected, we can trust the one who holds us in our hands. Because we can trust our Father, although we may feel weary and weak, we are never broken. God is with us through it all.

"A cheerful heart is good medicine, but a broken spirit saps a person's strength" (Proverbs 17:22).

DOLL CAMP

FOR MANY YEARS, MY MOTHER owned an antique doll business. Occasionally, while my mom was still collecting and selling, I would accompany her to some out-of-state doll conventions. Much to my mother's dismay, I didn't care much about the dolls, but I always found the doll collectors to be an interesting group.

Once, at a convention in Atlanta, I met my most memorable collector. I don't remember her name, but I can still see the enthusiasm on her face as she pressed some photos into my hand.

"Look," she said excitedly. "Look at these pictures. I sent a few of my dolls to camp, and the camp sent me these pictures. See her? Look, she is playing outside with the President Roosevelt doll. Isn't that fun?"

I did my best to act impressed and asked her a few questions. Yes, I discovered, there are people who *pay* to send their dolls to camp. You ship them, they attend "camp," and your reward is a stack of camp pictures.

I was in a state of shock. What a waste of money and time! What a ridiculous thing to do! But, seriously, don't we all invest money and time in ways that are wasteful? I can waste hours a day on things that don't matter. I can also put a lot of stock in things that don't mean a thing in the heavenly realm.

Although most of us don't have little idol statues sitting on our shelves, we all tend toward idols in our lives. It has been said that we can determine what our idols are by viewing our bank accounts, our calendars, and our phones' viewing histories. Ouch!

I may not send any dolls to camp, but I need to remember to camp on things that matter. Holy Spirit, show us the way!

> "Dear children, keep away from anything that might take God's place in your hearts" (1 John 5:21).

SILOS

IT WAS SPRING BREAK, AND we planned a trip to the Magnolia Silos in Waco. I pictured the kids romping playfully on the green, Mom and I contentedly looking on, and Emily peacefully strolling through the stores.

Here's how it really went: We had to pull off the freeway on the way there because Adrian would not stop screaming. He was very traumatized by being asked to turn the volume down on his movie, so it is, of course, understandable. And the promised accessible parking was nonexistent. Emily, Austin, and I had to carry Mom in her wheelchair like Cleopatra on a minion-powered throne across the bumpy, gravel parking lot.

When we were finally able to place Mom's wheelchair on smooth ground, we had to dodge in and out between people waiting in a line to enter the bakery. When I say *line*, I mean a queue of people wrapped around a very large building to pay vast amounts of money for a cupcake. My boggled mind felt even more boggled. We had one bit of good fortune. Despite a crowd that resembled one you would see at Disney World, all crammed into a much smaller space, Emily was able to enter one small shop without waiting in a line. Sadly, while sitting outside with the boys, another tragedy befell Adrian: his balloon popped, and he cried without pause for fifteen minutes. Soon, we realized that the food trucks were open. Hooray! Unfortunately, we immediately noticed that there was not *one* table open. Boo! We grabbed a park bench and held our ground.

As soon as we were seated, Mom gave a panicked cry for the toilet. A few minutes later, I was outside of her stall telling at least 108 women, that, "No, I'm not in line, I'm waiting for my mother." After a long, long, long, long time, my mother decided that she didn't need to go after all. Emily soon returned with a small bag containing $47.00 worth of food. The bag held five hamburgers and three lukewarm soft drinks in cans. No cookies. No chips. And, yes, $47.00!

After a short time, we decided to leave and go for ice cream at the shop that Emily had read about online. We wove our way through lots of traffic and arrived at the adorable little ice cream shop, but it was closed.

Fortunately, in the 1990s, I temporarily lost a neighbor child at Wet and Wild Water Park and experienced the worst hour of my life. So, at the end of our rotten day, I could at least say, "Well, it wasn't as bad the day the day I lost that kid at Wet and Wild."

In his book *The Enormous Exception*, Earl Palmer says that the secret to the durability of the Golden Gate Bridge is its firm foundation and flexibility. We got through the day at the silos by realizing that our foundation, the thing that really matters, is always firm. We also realized that we need to be able to flex. Big time. Always. Forever. And, of course … we need to laugh!

> "Anyone who listens to my teaching and follows it is wise, like a person who builds a house on solid rock" (Matthew 7:24).

PUZZLE

AUSTIN WAS EIGHT YEARS OLD, and we were in a little vacation rental two hours from home. He had been disappointed to realize that there were no horses to ride on the property, but he had made the best of things. He climbed trees, took joy in every rabbit sighting, and enjoyed swinging and singing in the worn-out swing. To his delight, he also found an old Carrier-brand air conditioning label made from hard plastic. In a wave of eight-year-old creativity, he broke the label into pieces and made them into a puzzle.

A little while later, we sat on the couch in the living room and a text came in from his aunt. "Look, Austin," I said. "Here's pictures of Huston and Arden with Uncle Clarke and Aunt Jennifer from their trip to Utah!" He marveled at the pictures of incredible landscapes and enjoyed seeing his cousins pictured on top of glorious mountains.

In typical happy fashion, Austin told me that he was glad his cousins got to be in Utah. Then he said, "And I am happy that I can be here, in this house, with my puzzle!"

I want to be like Austin. I want to be content with what I have and find joy in the smallest things. I don't want to compare. I want to be happy that I can be in here, in His house, with my Savior.

> **"Not that I was ever in need, for I have learned how to be content with whatever I have. I know how to live on almost nothing or with everything. I have** learned the secret of living in every situation, whether it is with a full stomach or empty, with plenty or little. For I can do everything through Christ, who gives me strength" (Philippians 4:11–13).

NO JEWELS

I WILL NOT RECEIVE ONE TEENY tiny, microscopic jewel in my crown for trusting God when my kids learned to drive. Mother worry reached its highest peak when my kids began to take the wheel. It didn't help that Clarke's first time riding in a car with another teen ended badly. The driver sped down the freeway so fast that he literally blew out his engine and they had to hike to a gas station.

So, picture me, at my peak of mother's worry, when a big, giant, tremendous storm blew into town one night. Clarke, who was sixteen at the time, worked at a grocery store in a small town about fifteen miles away and would be driving home in the dark and the pounding rain. Truitt, a typical dad, told me that Clarke would be OK and immediately fell asleep. Emily and I could not do the same. We both prayed and worried, prayed and worried on repeat.

When Clarke walked into the house that night, we felt that we could finally breathe! I asked Clarke how he managed on the road. He told me something that I've never forgotten. He said, "It's funny, Mom. But there was a car ahead of me the whole way home. I just followed the taillights of that car because I could not see the road." To this day, I believe that God used this car to guide Clarke.

Sometimes we are helpless. We cannot see our way. We cannot find the light. Remember, when your circumstances are dark, there is always a light. Reach out to God. Through His word. Through prayer. He is always reaching out to you.

> "Your word is a lamp to guide my feet and a light for my path" (Psalm 119:105).

MARA

ARA'S STORY AMAZES ME. SHE came to the United States from Mexico with her husband and five small children. She didn't speak a word of English, but soon took a job as a school-bus driver to help support her family. The only English phrase she knew was, "Sit down and be quiet." She was silenced by her inability to speak, but her spirit remained strong. Even as her husband abused her physically and emotionally, she refused to give up. She was a mother who wanted good things for her children, so she learned English and learned to survive.

One day, someone from a local church knocked on Mara's door and told her about Jesus Christ and how He died on the cross for her. She learned that He wanted to be her Savior. In an instant, He became just that. Mara's eyes were opened, and her strength became the amazing strength of the Lord. Even in the darkness of her marriage, Mara's felt the joy and passion for Christ Jesus. She longed to know more about God's word and found herself sneaking out the bathroom window with her kids in tow to go to church. Her husband would never approve, but she cared more about her Savior.

Years later, when I worked in ministry at our church, Mara worked in the facilities department, cleaning the children's building with tender love and care. Her official job name, unlike mine, did not have the word *minister* in the title. But she ministered to more people than I ever even imagined ministering to. Every place Mara went, and every place she goes to this day, is her place of ministry. She shares the gospel at Costco. She shares the gospel at the bank. She hosts Bible clubs for kids in Mexico as many times as year as is possible.

But Mara's greatest passion is "her homeless." She feeds many, many people on the street each week. She always makes sure that they hear the gospel as well. One Sunday, Mara called me crying and crying. My heart dropped. Had someone died? No, Mara was sad because an arctic storm had prevented her from driving her car to feed her people. Her passion is so strong that she cannot stand to be thwarted for even one day.

Had it been me, I would have thought, *Oh, well. I will catch them next week.* Not Mara. There is a passion and strength in her that will not be stopped. Mara is my greatest hero, and she spurs me on. She is the greatest minister that I know.

Do you have someone in your life that spurs you on? Do you spur anyone on? We need each other.

> "Let us think of ways to motivate one another to acts of love and good works" (Hebrews 10:24).

GIFTS

ONE OF THE *STRANGEST* GIFTS I ever received was from my grandmother. It was my eleventh birthday, and I opened my brightly wrapped present to find a box of Kleenex. You could be thinking that this was a joke and that there was money hidden in the box, but no. It was a box of Kleenex. I knew that my grandmother loved me, but I also knew that she was not mentally stable, so I was able to thank her politely and laugh to myself inside. One of the most *touching* gifts I ever received was from my friend Carla. I was pregnant with Clarke when she appeared on my doorstep on Mother's Day with a card and bouquet of honeysuckles from her garden. What makes this story even more touching is that she had recently lost her fiancé in a plane crash. That she could celebrate me while she was in such pain was astounding and was an act of love that I have never forgotten.

I often ask God to help me to be more like Carla. I want to rejoice with those who rejoice and mourn with those who mourn. Sadly, we are prone to envying those who rejoice and forgetting those who mourn. I suspect that in heaven, we will be filled with incredible, amazing love for one another. If we could be filled with even a bit of that selfless, caring love on earth, I think we would have a small taste of heavenly joy. I'm going to keep praying for that kind of love!

> "Be happy with those who are happy, and weep with those who weep" (Romans 12:15).

CAN'T WANT TO!

WHEN OUR GRANDSON AUSTIN WAS a toddler, he developed the usual two-year-old word *no* into a complex and insightful phrase. He used it, for example, when he locked himself in the bathroom stall at church.

"Austin," I pleaded. "Unlock that door and come out right now."

Echoing from the confines of the four walls, I heard his cheerful and definite reply, "Can't want to!" Believe me, Austin found countless opportunities to use these words.

Sadly, I use these words a lot as well. I don't say them out loud, but I hear them loudly and clearly in my own head and heart. Here's a great volunteer opportunity! "Can't want to." Here's a great chance for Christian community! "Can't want to." Here's a chance to use your talents! "Can't want to." Here's a perfect opportunity for prayer and Bible study! "Can't want to." Here's a great opportunity to share the gospel! "Can't want to."

Sometimes we must move forward even when we "can't want to." Moving forward in community, in serving, and in praying, reading the Bible, and sharing God's truths when we have no desire to do so, is a great act of faith. Not only is it an act of faith, but moving forward strengthens the faith!

Wise believer knows that is sometimes best to say no. There are times when we need breaks and times when life's situations limit our abilities to do all we would like to do. But a wise believer also knows not to shut the door to the vital nutrients of growing in and serving the Lord. Lord, Help us *want to*! Amen.

> "So let's not get tired of doing what is good. At just the right time we will reap a harvest of blessing if we don't give up" (Galatians 6:9).

SMOKY

Poor Smoky. Truitt's family adopted that wild little Chihuahua when my husband was in middle school. Smoky did not realize that he was small. He was, however, quite sure that he was fierce and just the kind of dog that the ladies would love.

One day, Smoky escaped the house to pursue a courtship with a neighboring dog. The other male dogs in the area did not approve. They demonstrated their disapproval in the way that dogs in this situation often do, and Smoky was chomped, chewed, and unceremoniously kicked out of the way. He made it home, but he was severely wounded.

"Wrap him up," Truitt's dad said, "If he makes it, he makes it. If he doesn't …" Remarkably, tough little Smoky pulled through.

However, the removal of the adhesive bandages took every bit of fur from Smoky's body, and it never grew back. When I met Smoky in 1971, I thought that he was the ugliest dog that I had ever seen. His eyes bulged, and his bald skin was covered with gnarled warts. As if that wasn't bad enough, he yelped incessantly and stunk up the room. If there had been a contest for the world's most flatulent dog, Smoky would have come home with the biggest trophy!

But you know what? The Rogers family loved that little dog. He didn't look like a dog that deserved to be loved, and he didn't act like a dog that deserved to be loved. Yet, he was.

That's us, you know. We don't deserve to be loved. Compared to God's goodness and greatness, we are nothing. Our human nature is stinky and ugly, and even the fiercest of us cannot win the fight to be like God. That's why God sent Jesus. When we believe in Him and receive Him as Savior, we are accepted as God's much-loved children. He is our Father who never stops loving us.

Thank God! Literally!

> "God saved you by his grace when you believed. And you can't take credit for this; it is a gift from God. Salvation is not a reward for the good things we have done, so none of us can boast about it" (Ephesian 2:8–9).

THAT LOG!

*W*HEN YOU CARE FOR SOMEONE with dementia, it is easy to fall into the trap of being condescending. My mother very kindly shook me out of that pattern one morning at breakfast. I sat her down with a nice cup of coffee and her morning meds. I made my own coffee and began to heartily chomp down my own breakfast. I was devouring my granola bar while reading the morning devotional when I noticed my mother pointing.

"What's the matter, Mom?" I asked, wondering why she was stopping me midsentence. Didn't she know that God's word is important? "Is that my toast in the oven?" she asked politely.

Yes. I had begun to eat my own breakfast and forgotten to give my mom her food.

I apologized, and she said, "That's ok, honey. We all forget sometimes."

At that point, my mom had no short-term memory, but she did remember to be kind. Was I that patient with her? I hoped so. I prayed so.

Remembering my own occasional forgetfulness humbled me. We so often look at other's weaknesses and forget our own. It is easy to see the sins of the people around us and forget our own weaknesses. Occasionally, I think of all of the people in my life and ask God to show me my own sins toward each person. I am shocked when He reveals bad attitudes, anger, or envy that is weighing down my spirit. This exercise is painful, yet it is amazingly revitalizing and refreshing. Try it!

The log in our own eyes can be real!

> **"And why worry about a speck in your friend's eye when you have a log in your own? How can you think of saying to your friend, 'Let me help you get rid of that speck in your eye,' when you can't see past the log in your own eye?** Hypocrite! First get rid of the log in your own eye, then you will see well enough to deal with the speck in your friend's eye" (Matthew 7:3–5).

BUSY

I ONCE ASKED MY FRIEND PENNY about her mother-in-law. "She is in assisted living now," Penny told me. "Every time we talk to her, she tells us that she is pretty busy."

"That's good," I said and smiled.

"You know how she spends her days?" Penny asked. "She gets up in the morning, goes down to breakfast, and then goes back to her room to pray. She then goes to lunch and spends the afternoon praying as well. After dinner, she watches TV and goes to bed."

What a great way to be busy! Penny's mother-in-law understood something very important. She understood that there is more to life than rushing from place to place, staying physically busy, and getting tasks done.

She understood that praying was an incredibly important way to spend her days. I can't even imagine the impact that her prayers have made in the lives of her family, her church, and our entire community over the years.

There are seasons in our lives when we cannot volunteer, cannot do physical tasks, cannot attend church or host Bible studies in our home. There are seasons when we are ill or homebound for other various reasons. Yet, we can always pray. Praying is the most sacred of tasks. We won't receive rewards for it. We won't be noticed for it. We won't receive applause. But we will see amazing things happen in our lives and in our hearts.

Let's stay busy in prayer. Let's find strength and peace in time with our Father.

> "Rejoice in our confident hope. Be patient in trouble and keep on praying" (Romans 12:12).

THE CAKE

SIXTEENTH BIRTHDAYS SEEM SPECIAL. WHEN that birthday was on the horizon for Emily, Truitt was shooting photography for a popular arts-and-crafts publication. During a photo shoot, he met a baker from Europe who had created some incredible cakes for the magazine. He came home raving about her beautiful creations, and we decided to hire her to make a cake for Emily's special birthday. The price would be more than we usually spent, but a sixteenth birthday is very special!

Emily decided on a secret garden theme, and Truitt carefully spelled out the details to the renowned cake artist, who carefully took down detailed notes. We could hardly wait to see her creation! The party day arrived, and Emily's friends gathered at the skating rink that we had rented for her big day. We had raved about the special baker, and all her friends eagerly anticipated Truitt's arrival with the cake. We were shocked when he plopped down a cake from the local grocery store on the table. Then he told the story. When he had picked up the cake at the bakery, he was stunned. The cake could only be described as hideous. The secret garden was an unattractive olive green, and it looked like a five-year-old had done the decoration. Truitt was too shocked to speak, so he paid and left the store.

In his desperation, he stopped by Albertsons and headed toward the bakery. All the baker employees were on break. However, a young grocery store employee who had never decorated a cake in his life said he would write a birthday greeting on a plain cake and decorate it as best as he could. It looked amazing!

After admiring the grocery store cake, we all gasped when Truitt opened the box to reveal the original cake. It was unbelievably ugly. We had a lot of fun trying to figure out what had happened and laughing at the muddy looking "secret garden." We never knew why the baker had created such an ugly cake, but we did learn that sometimes the experts fail and the inexperienced can come through! The young man at the grocery store was unafraid and eager to serve! Help me, God, to be like that as I look toward the roles you have for me, unafraid and eager to serve!

> "For I hold you by your right hand—I, the Lord you God.
> And, I say to you, 'Don't be afraid. I am here to help you'"
> (Isaiah 41:13).

WONDER

WHEN I RETIRED FROM MINISTRY, my friend Debbie was delighted. "I hope that this time without constant stress and heavy schedules will allow you to regain your sense of wonder," she told me.

I thought about that a lot. I couldn't recall the last time that I felt true and pure wonder. Pondering what wonder really meant, I remembered my shy third-grader self. I pictured the fat hungry silkworms.

Those of us in Mrs. Krauss's third grade class who had mulberry trees in our yard were allowed to take turns bringing the class silkworms home for the weekend. I was delighted when my weekend as caterpillar sitter finally arrived. On Saturday, I watched them munch their leaves and travel around and around the shoebox. On Sunday, something spectacular happened. The caterpillars began to spin their cocoons. I was filled with awe and true wonder at God's design of these amazing creatures. Not only was it a joy and a delight to see the magical spinning, but it was happening at my house while I was on duty. I was ecstatic.

Because I was so full of wonder, I forgot to be shy. When my mom suggested that we call my teacher, I didn't hesitate. I got on the phone and excitedly gave Mrs. Krauss a play-by-play account of the silkworms and their spinning. I surprised myself. Phone calls were usually very difficult for me. Yet, it was the wonder that propelled me. Wonder made me forgot my shyness. Wonder filled me up with real joy.

As we age, it is easy to lose our sense of wonder. We look at the beautiful sunrise, enjoy it for a few moments, and then get back to mentally ticking off our to-do lists. The burdens of life can so easily weigh down our spirits and diminish our abilities to enjoy the simple, incredible things that God puts in our paths. I believe that the Holy Spirit can help us regain the wonder that is so easily lost. I believe that wonder propels us forward and gives us hope.

Sometimes, I admit, I feel no joy. I feel no wonder. In those times, I ask God to restore me. He hears. He provides. Wonder is wonderful! Don't give up on it.

"For you are great and perform wonderful deeds. You alone are God" (Psalm 86:10).

KNOWN

TRUITT WAS ONCE ASKED TO do the photography for a coffee table book about Nolan Ryan. Truitt had the famous pitcher at his studio for photos and found him to be a very down-to-earth and likeable man. However, the brief time at Truitt's studio did not make Truitt and Nolan real friends. This came to light clearly one day when the book publisher asked Truitt to drive to Nolan's ranch house to take photos of his trophy case. At first, things went well. Truitt was greeted by Nolan's father-in-law, who welcomed him into the house and showed him the trophies.

Then the phone rang. Truitt heard the alarm in his host's voice. Soon, he was hearing profuse apologies. He knew what was coming. Sure enough, the father-in-law returned, red-faced and agitated. "You will have to leave," he told Truitt. "Nolan says that he did not give permission for you to be here." Oops.

Truitt graciously left, of course, and now jokes that he has been thrown out of some of the best places. The Nolan Ryan story is funny. Truitt didn't get the photos he needed, but in the long run, it didn't matter.

What does matter is eternity. When I read Matthew 7:22–23, I am filled with incredible relief and joy in understanding that Jesus knows me and will let me in His house on judgment day. Not everyone will be welcome. If you know Jesus, fall on your knees and thank Him now that you will have access into His kingdom. If you do not, simply ask Jesus to be your Savior right now. Believe him and receive him into your life. It is that simple. Romans 10:9 says, "If you openly declare that Jesus is Lord and believe in your heart that God raised him from the dead, you will be saved." The will of our Father is for us to accept Jesus as Savior. He wants to welcome us into His house. For those of us who know Him, the door will be opened wide. What joy!

"On judgment day many will say to me, 'Lord, Lord!
We prophesied in your name and cast out demons

in your name and performed many miracles in your name.' But I will reply, 'I never knew you. Get away from me, you who break God's laws'" (Matthew 7:22–23).

"If you openly declare that Jesus is Lord and believe in your heart that God raised him from the dead, you will be saved" (Romans 10:9).

NOT SO SUPERPOWER

OUR KIDS GREW UP WATCHING old black-and-white movies. Truitt and I loved them and considered them safe to view with children. However, when Clarke was in the fifth grade, he made a case for bringing some contemporary films into the Friday-night movie mix. We agreed, and Truitt selected an action movie. We sat in the TV room watching the movie, and I really enjoyed it. However, I could not quite relax. I was anxious about possible inappropriate scenes popping up, so I kept my hand on the remote.

Sure enough, a scene opened at a soldier's birthday celebration, and a large cake was rolled in. And yes, just as you have probably guessed, a barely clad girl soon jumped out of the cake. But I didn't worry! I had my trusty remote, kind of like a superpower, and I was going to protect our family from evil! I pushed the button. But instead of pushing fast-forward, I accidentally pushed pause. Then I became so flustered, I consistently pushed pause and replay over and over instead of fast-forward. Because of my fruitless efforts to protect them, our kids saw the cake woman about four or five times longer than the original scene length in the movie! My remote superpower was not a superpower at all.

As we view the news each day, we see evil a lot worse than a girl jumping out of a cake. We wish we had superpowers so we could stop it. In our dark moments, we feel hopeless and as though any efforts to change things would be useless. On our own, of course, we *are* useless. But God *has the superpower*! When we see evil seemingly win around us, we can read God's word and understand that our Father told us evil would be part of our lives on earth. He also told us that it would increase as the time for Christ's return drew near. We hate it. We hate it for our children. We hate it for our grandchildren.

We can't stop evil, but we are not powerless. Let's draw on the power of God and spread the gospel to the world. It is our hope against evil. God's power is the strength we need to spread this marvelous hope!

MELINDA ROGERS

"For I am not ashamed of this Good News about Christ. It is the power of God at work, saving everyone who believes-the Jew first and also the Gentile. This Good News tells us how God makes us right in his sight. This is accomplished from start to finish by faith. As the Scriptures say, 'It is through faith that a righteous person has life'" (Romans1:16–17).

EARL

$\mathcal{E}$ ARL TOMERLIN WAS A BIG man. He was big in stature, big in personality, and big in heart. I met Earl when I started my first full-time job at General Dynamics Corporation. I was hired as a stenographer for a group of employees who had worked there for years. I was among the first of the new staff hired after several years of employee cutbacks. Consequently, there was a large age gap between me and almost everyone else in the company.

I felt like a child and probably looked like one to most everyone there. Earl, a faithful Baptist and strong family man, took me under his wing. He gave me marriage advice and, when I found out that I was expecting Clarke, took me to meet his wife for parenting wisdom. Yet, the most important lesson I learned from Earl was the importance of accepting the generosity of others. This lesson was learned through coffee.

Day after day, Earl would stop by my desk on his way to the coffee vending machine and ask if he could buy me a cup. I always declined. His face always fell. Then one day, I decided to put an end to Earl's sad face.

"Yes," I said. "Buy me a cup!"

Earl smiled the biggest smile, and from that day forward, I never declined his offer to buy me ten-cent cups of horrible, bitter office vending machine coffee. My acceptance of his kind offer made Earl very, very happy, and it warmed my own heart as well. To this day, when I receive an offer or help and my pride or sense of self-sufficiency pops up like a large foreboding wall, I think of Earl. Sometimes we need to accept the generosity of others. Sometimes we can't do it alone. Sometimes we just need a simple cup of love from a friend.

"Share each other's burdens, and in this way obey the law of Christ" (Galatians 6:2).

FOR SALE

*T*RUITT ONCE RECEIVED A PHOTOGRAPHY assignment in Vidalia, Georgia. He decided to drive, and I decided to accompany him on the trip. We really enjoyed stopping at small, out-of-the-way places and taking in the southern countryside.

As we drove down a country highway one morning, we saw something very curious. A beautiful vintage car was parked under an awning near the road. We were shocked at the sign above the car. For Sale, $1400.00. We sped by, too shocked to take in the enormity of the bargain we had just seen.

That night in our hotel room, Truitt brought up the car. "We have just got to check that car out," he said. "I've always wanted a vintage car, and that price is unbelievable!"

So, instead of taking the shortest way home, we backtracked on the back roads of Georgia in search of the car. After a morning of driving and a big sigh of relief, we found the car still parked in the same spot. We made our way to the modest farmhouse and knocked on the door.

"I'm interested in buying your car," Truitt told the nice gentleman who answered the door. We sauntered outside, and the man began show us the meticulous remodeling details and beautiful features of the car.

After several minutes, he ended his description of all the work he had done and said, "I will take fourteen thousand for it."

Truitt and I looked at each other in shock. "Uh," Truitt stammered. "But your sign says fourteen *hundred*."

The man burst out laughing. "Oh, that," he said. "That's for the awning!"

Truitt and I had assumed that the cost of the car was very low. We had to have it! Yet, the cost was greater than we ever expected.

Haven't we all paid the costs for giving in to temptations or for making bad decisions because we have failed to count the costs? The bright and shiny things that so often call our names are not worth the cost. Pray first, move slow, and let God show you the way!

> "And don't let us yield to temptation but rescue us from the evil one" (Matthew 6:13).

SQUEEZED

MY FRIEND DEB IS A nurse. One day in a barbecue restaurant in Houston, her nursing skills were put to a frightening test. Deb and a group of friends had just finished their meal when she noticed something alarming. The son of one of her dining companions was turning blue and grabbing wildly at his throat. The five-year-old looked panicked but could not utter a sound. He was choking.

Deb's training clicked in, and she began the Heimlich maneuver. Over and over, she performed rigorous abdominal thrusts to dislodge the obstruction. After a disturbing period, the unknown object so cruelly stuck in the young boy's throat showed no signs of moving. Her mind began to race. Could she do an impromptu tracheotomy? Would that be the only option? Fortunately, that decision did not have to be made. Before long, one of the thrusts pushed a large peppermint candy out of the child's mouth, and he began to breathe again.

The parents, who had been watching in wide-eyed horror, grabbed up their son and thanked God that their boy was taking in the wonderful gift of oxygen. Relief. Relief. Relief.

In the car on the way home, the child's mother asked her son if he understood what Deb had done. "Yes!" he said, bursting out in a deep, heartfelt wail. "She was squeezing me to death!"

Have you ever felt like that? I have.

In 2013, our second grandson suffered a traumatic brain injury during birth, our daughter-in-law was diagnosed with breast cancer, my father-in-law passed away, and my mother had a major stroke. I felt like I was being squeezed to death. That year, I often sat at my desk staring at the computer and pretending to work. Sometimes I could pray, and sometimes I could not. I could barely comprehend the pain, let alone deal with it.

When I could, I cried out to God. I knew that He was there. I knew that He cared even if my heart seemed frozen inside of me. The squeezing was hard and horrible, yet many obstructions were removed from me. The things that really and truly mattered in life became much clearer and dearer. Frivolities and vanities lost their appeal. I saw God's hand moving in incredible, life-changing ways.

We grow more like Christ when we are being squeezed. We hold on tighter to Christ when we are at the end of ourselves. Just like the young boy who didn't understand that the painful thrusts into his small abdomen were saving his life, we don't understand the difficult, terrible things that sometimes come our way. But God knows. He is our lifesaver, our breath-giver, and our hero. Let's trust Him. He knows. He cares. He is God.

> **"So after you have suffered for a little while, he will restore, support, and** strengthen you, and he will place you on a firm foundation" (1 Peter 5:10b).

KUMQUATS

*I*T WAS A GLOOMY MORNING in Amarillo, Texas. Truitt, Arden, and I woke in our hotel room with our next stop, Red River, New Mexico, on our minds. We made our way down the hotel elevator to the line of sleepy-looking people in line for the breakfast buffet. No one was smiling. No one was talking. It was the end stage of the first major COVID pandemic, and some people were wearing masks. Some were not. Tension was in the air.

The server handed Truitt his waffles and asked if he needed anything else. In his loud and booming voice, Truitt replied, "Got any kumquats?" Everyone's heads whipped around, and smiles appeared on the formerly glum faces. The kumquat dialogue continued for several minutes, and even the manager joined in.

"I'm sure that I can whip up some kumquat puree for your waffles," he said, laughing.

Humor is such a gift. It shifts our moods and reminds us that there is still joy in this difficult world. Humor is the medicine of hope and comfort. When Emily moved to Tennessee is a young woman, she packed a stack of our Dick Van Dyke–show DVDs in her overloaded suitcase. They brought her a lot of comfort as she acclimated to her new city. When she laughed at something that Rob said to Buddy, the warm memories of laughing together at the same show as a family would wrap around her like a warm blanket.

We often hear about the benefits of crying. Article after article warns us that holding negative feelings in is detrimental to our health. Ironically, we seldom read about the benefits of laughing. I truly believe that exercising our "funny bones" is a vital, life-changing workout. Don't hold back. Laugh at something. Smile. There is joy in this difficult world.

"A cheerful heart is good medicine, but a broken spirit saps a person's strength" (Proverbs 17:22).

BURIED SWEATERS

HEN THE KIDS WERE IN elementary school, I went to a garage sale and came home with a Dalmatian! Perdy was very loved and probably one of the greatest garage sale finds in the history of our family. Unlike some dogs in her breed, Perdy was calm, sweet, and passive. Yet, it was many years before we realized that the term "passive aggressive" might have been a better description of our tricky garage sale dog.

Each winter, we purchased a warm sweater for Perdy. Each year, we would place the sweater on her lanky back and deem her adorable and warm. We were always very pleased. But each year, shortly after our sweater purchases, Perdy would meet us at the back door, looking innocent and mysteriously bare-backed. Where in the world did her sweaters go? We were perplexed. Then, one year I decided to dig a flowerbed that took up about a quarter of the yard. I dug up lots of dirt, roots, and, yes, several dog sweaters. Somehow, Perdy had managed each year to strip the sweater off her back and bury it safely under the dirt. She was just too cool for cute sweaters! Out of sight and out of mind, she must have reasoned.

We can all be like Perdy, can't we? Maybe we have a snag in a relationship, and we need to go to the person who has something against us as directed in Matthew 5:23. Yet somehow, we find that it is easier to hide behind busyness or excuses. Maybe we say yes to people when we need to say *no* because it is easier that way. Then again, maybe we say no when we should say yes because we find it easier to bury ourselves in our corners.

When I read about Jesus's time on earth, I see that he had two incredible traits we seldom see together. Jesus was loving, and at the same time, he was forthright. He did not play games. He loved mightily and spoke the truth without equivocation. Truth and love. What a combination!

"All you need is a simple yes or no; anything beyond that comes from the evil one" (Matthew 5:37).

OUT OF CONTROL

ONE FRIDAY AFTERNOON, I FOUND myself in Walmart doing our weekly grocery shopping. Emily called, and we were cheerfully chatting when I felt a strange sensation. I felt the skin on the side of my face and on my chin begin to tingle. Then, even more disconcertingly, I felt my skin moving. I tried to describe the strange development to Emily, but soon said goodbye and headed to the mirror at the sunglasses station. My eyes widened as I saw what was happening. Even as I watched, my face broke out into angry red bumps. I felt totally stunned and out of control. I felt a little bit like the Wolfman turning from man into wolf without any way to stop the change.

The mystery rash plagued me all weekend, especially when I had to lead a teacher training with a swollen red face. After my presentation, my boss looked at my face and said, "Boy, you were brave to get up there looking like that!" (Was that a compliment? I'm still not sure about that one!) Yet, I survived the ordeal and received my diagnosis at the doctor's office on Monday: poison ivy. I learned that poison ivy is systemic and can pop out anywhere on your body once you are exposed. I was prescribed steroids, and the itchy, burning mass finally went away.

Sometimes we just do not have control. Sometimes we are happily heading in one direction, and then something very unexpected and terrible pops up and blocks our way. We find that as we go through life, there are days that start out normally and end up leaving us devastated. Have you ever laid in your bed at night and wondered how things could change so quickly for the worse? I certainly have. Once, when facing difficult changes, I jotted down these lines in my journal: "I move but my world doesn't change. I try but things stay the same. I cannot move mountains, I can't rearrange. All my hope is in You."

Of course, as believers, we know that God walks with us through all these surprises. We also know that nothing surprises Him. Even though we don't know in advance when life will make a disheartening U-turn,

God knows. Not only does He know. He cares. He is the doctor we turn to. He is mighty.

> "I have told you all this so that you may have peace in me. Here on earth you will have many trials and sorrows. But take heart because I have overcome the world" (John 16:33).

APPLAUSE

ONE SUMMER DAY, I WAS running errands and decided to visit a small discount store before heading home. I shopped for a few minutes, found a couple of items to purchase, and headed to the checkout desk.

"Would you like to donate some money toward children in need?" the cashier asked.

I said yes and pressed the dollar donation button. Suddenly, everything stopped. The cashier grabbed a microphone and made an announcement that additional money had been collected for the children! Before I could really understand what was happening, employees throughout the store were shouting and applauding.

I simply stood at the counter with a dazed and slightly embarrassed look on my face. All of this for a dollar donation? But as it turns out, the amazing moment of celebratory jubilation was not my only reward. Because I had so very generously donated a dollar, I was presented with a paper that would allow me five dollars off my next purchase.

I was overcelebrated. Yet, my experience there made me ponder the times that we are undercelebrated. Those times occur almost every day. I thought about the parent changing the tenth smelly diaper of the day. I thought about the adult son or daughter trimming the toenails of his or her elderly parent. I thought about the schoolteacher who chose making a difference in the lives of students rather than making a large amount of money. There is no applause for the day-to-day things that can be challenging, difficult, or mundane. Yet, when we study Jesus's life, we see clearly that He did not live for applause. He lived for and died for others.

Ukraine pastor Benjamin Morrison placed this quote on his Facebook page while in the middle of helping refugees find shelter and resources on their way out of the country: "We don't serve others for the gratitude we get from them, but out of gratitude for what Christ has done for us." When we follow His lead, we can be content doing hard things without applause. Serving our amazing Father is reward enough.

MELINDA ROGERS

"Love your enemies! Do good to them. Lend to them without expecting to be repaid. Then your reward from heaven will be very great, and you will truly be acting as children of the Most High, for he is kind to those who are unthankful and wicked" (Luke 6:35).

RIVER

I CAN STILL PICTURE EMILY IN her gray corduroy coat with red trim. Her chubby three-year-old legs were moving full speed ahead as she, Clarke, my dad, and I enjoyed a day on the trail at the park. The trail ran alongside a river, and my mother radar was on high alert. As preschoolers often do, Emily ran ahead of us and soon began to make her way off the trail and onto the bank.

"Emily," my dad and I shouted simultaneously, "come back here. You are going to fall in the river."

To this day, we laugh about Emily's classic preschooler reaction. She whipped her head around, looked at us reproachfully, and said, "I'm not going to fall in the r-i-v - e-r ..."

Her last word was drawn out and took on a pathetic tone as she tumbled down the bank and into the water. The water was not deep, but Emily cried from the wet and the cold as we hauled her up and ran her back to the car.

We have recounted that story over and over at family gatherings, and everyone laughs. But the story always reminds me of the times when I have not listened to my own Father, my heavenly one, and have gone my own way. I, too, have ended up in the cold and needing rescue. Yet, my Father doesn't give up on me. If you have accepted Christ as your Savior, you, too, can rest in knowing that your Father loves you no matter what. When we call on Him, He scoops us up, loves us, teaches us, and gives us direction. He forgives us and allows us to warm ourselves by the warmth of His light.

> "Listen! The Lord's arm is not too weak to save you, nor is
> his ear too deaf to hear you call" (Isaiah 59:1).

STAND UP

ECEMBER IN 1987 WAS A month of difficult days. I went for a routine pregnancy sonogram and was told that I had a large mass. My obstetrician told me that it was important to schedule immediate surgery to rule out the possibility of cancer. Even though sunlight streamed in through our windows as it always had, I felt as if the light had been dimmed. I felt terrible darkness. As it happened, I did not have cancer, but we lost our third child. And sadly, our surprise pregnancy turned into an unplanned hysterectomy as the large cyst was removed.

My surgery took place at a new hospital that was extremely understaffed. Kerry, a dear friend and a nurse, kept checking on me by phone and became unhappy about the lack of care and response that I was experiencing.

Shortly after one of my phone calls with Kerry, I looked out my window and saw someone moving with great determination across the parking lot. As the person got closer, I saw that it was Kerry. I will never forget the "I've got a mission" look on her face or the purple velvet pants that she was wearing. Kerry strode up to the nurses' station and kindly but firmly told them that I needed some assistance. A few minutes later she was in my room, comforting me and telling me what she had done. Nurses soon flocked into my room and were suddenly offering all kinds of help.

Kerry was my advocate. I knew that she cared for me because she acted on my behalf. Jesus told us that when we care for others, we are also caring for Him. I pray that I can truly care of others like Jesus cared. People who stand up for us when we are down are bright lights in a dark world. Lord, help me to stand.

> **"Speak up for those who cannot speak for themselves; ensure justice for those being crushed. Yes, speak up for the poor and helpless,** and see that they get justice" (Proverbs 31:8–9).

GAUGE

*T*RUITT ONCE HAD A SERIES of jobs with an architectural firm that required him to book planes and helicopters for aerial photography all over the country. I worked for Truitt at the time and did my best to find reputable pilots to fill the need. Most of the pilots I booked were excellent. Most of the helicopters and planes were in good condition. And then there was the guy in Denver. Oh my.

Truitt met the young pilot at the airport, and he seemed excited and eager to fly Truitt to Wyoming. Truitt, however, seemed a little less eager when he spied the helicopter. It was not on the cutting edge of helicopter excellence. It looked, in fact, a little shabby. Yet, things went swimmingly. Truitt got the needed shots in Wyoming and felt relaxed and confident as they headed back to Colorado. He felt relaxed, that is, until the pilot told him to be on the lookout for a good place to land.

"Why do we need to land?" Truitt asked. "We are nowhere near Denver."

"Oh, I think I'm out of gas."

"Don't you have a gas gauge?"

"Nah. That thing hasn't worked in years."

So, within a few scary moments, they found themselves landed in a cornfield. The pilot stuck a stick in the gas tank and decided that they had plenty of gas. Truitt was relieved as there are not a lot of places to fuel a helicopter in a cornfield!

Gauges are very important. God's word is a gauge for believers. When we read the Bible, we can tell where we are, where we are going and just what we need. We can see our flaws and find ways to fill up with God's presence. God's word is a gauge that *always* works! We simply need to put it into action.

"For the word of God is alive and powerful. It is sharper than the sharpest two-edged sword, cutting between soul and spirit, between joint and marrow. It exposes our innermost thoughts and desires" (Hebrews 4:12).

CAMPING

W E HAVE A LOT OF great memories of camping with several families from our church as the kids were growing up. Jaymes was known as the tarp king. He could build a whole village out of tarps. Ruth was a minimalist who brought a lot of great conversation to the campsite, but very few supplies. Like a mystical wizard, Kenny could lure a fish onto his line with the flick of his flashlight on the water in the lake. Each of the friends we camped with has his or her own special place in our camping memories hall of fame. Julie and Ken Miller get the award for attaining the perfect camping tableau. It is etched in my mind and always makes me laugh.

We arrived at the state park on a cloudy Friday evening with our trusty tent in tow. The Millers had arrived about an hour before us and had their cozy pop-up trailer in place and ready to go. We greeted each other with hugs and excitement. The Millers were preparing to eat dinner, so we nixed their offer to help us put up our tent.

"Clarke and I can do it," Truitt assured them. We hauled the tent bag out of the SUV and went to work.

As soon as the tent pieces were laid out on the ground there was a peal of thunder. Within seconds, an unbelievable amount of heavy, torrential rain began to pour from the sky. All the family pitched in, and we tried our best to get the tent in place. We scrambled, heaved, twisted, and tried our best to get the poles in the ground. It was difficult to see anything in the blinding rain, but I will never forget looking over at the Millers' trailer. While we were being pelted with cold bullets of rain, they were sitting peacefully in their screened-in pop-up, smiling, laughing, and enjoying a delicious home cooked meal. The contrast was hilarious!

Although this straight-out-of-a sitcom scenario made me laugh, other types of contrasts can be difficult. When we are suffering financially, or with our health, relationships, or any other type of pain, it can be difficult to see others seemingly enjoying life. Those contrasts are *hard*.

It is always helpful to remember that our suffering is part of our unique story, and that God is the author. A time of suffering is a time to call on God. Sometimes all we able say is, "Help me, Jesus!" And that's OK.

When I call out to Jesus, I remember that my suffering is never anything compared to the suffering He went through for us. That is a contract I cannot comprehend.

> "He was despised and rejected-a man of sorrows, acquainted with deepest grief. We turned our back on him and looked the other way. He was despised and we did not care" (Isaiah 53:3).

HEAD FREEZE

MY HUSBAND GETS A KICK out of my rain preparedness. If there is the slightest bit of precipitation in the forecast, I make sure my hooded raincoat goes with me in the car. If there is a big chance of rain, my giant umbrella goes with me as well. Yet, during my middle-school years, I would not go near a raincoat, umbrella, or hat. For some incredible reason, it was considered social suicide to take any of those items, so loved by our parents, to the bus stop.

I remember the perplexed and frustrated look on my mom's face. "You mean you had rather get soaked than carry an umbrella?"

"Yes," I replied without equivocation.

Raincoats, umbrellas, and hats were just not acceptable. At all. Under any circumstance, ever.

My neighbor, Carrie, understood this as well. Unfortunately, he did not understand the implications of washing his hair and heading straight to the bus stop on one of the coldest mornings of the year.

Yes. His head froze. He stood hatless at the bus stop with white, frozen hair twinkling in the morning sunlight. We all laughed, and the boys teased him good-naturedly. At least his parents had not forced him to wear the dreaded hat! Frozen heads were, without a doubt, MUCH more acceptable!

My middle school refusal to take the tools my parents offered me to the school each day reminds me of our natural inclination toward the tools that God gives us. Get up early to pray and read the Bible? Oh, man. That's not cool. I don't need those tools. Uh, yes. We do. We need those tools more than raincoats, umbrellas, and hats. We need those tools to set our course and lighten our spirits. If we refuse the amazing tools of spiritual growth and help that God offers, we end up with more than frozen heads. We end up with frozen hearts. A frozen heart listens to lies and moves away from God. Warm up and protect yourself each day with His word and His directing presence.

> "The spirit alone gives eternal life. Human effort accomplishes nothing. And the very words I have spoken to you are spirit and life" (John 6:63).

TEDDY RUXPIN

O NE SUNDAY MORNING, I SAUNTERED down the hallway of our church's children's building, stopping at each classroom to see if the teachers needed supplies or help of any kind. I was a volunteer at the time, and my job was to help the classroom leaders in any way that I could.

As I passed by the rows of classrooms, my heart was touched by the groups of children gathered around their teachers, listening to God's word. And then, I heard something very different. I stopped outside the classroom with the unusual sounds and saw a strange sight. Like all the other classrooms, the children were gathered into a circle listening to their teacher. Except in this case, the teacher was Teddy Ruxpin, the talking teddy bear. The human teacher was not at all engaged with the kids and was allowing Teddy Ruxpin to tell them a story that had nothing to do with God's word.

On one level, it worked. The children were delighted and were, indeed, hearing a story. But two key elements were missing: There was no relationship or truth being shared. The teacher had pawned off her relationship responsibilities to a toy. The story being told was not harmful, but time that could have been used to teach the children from God's word was wasted. Too often, we can miss those two elements in our own lives. "I don't need to serve in that ministry. I send them money, for Pete's sake." "I don't want to talk to Jason about the Bible. He doesn't want to hear about that. I'll just send him one from Amazon. Credit card in action and problem solved!"

Service that is done out of obligation and with the least amount of giving of ourselves makes little impact. On the other hand, true service that is driven by the Holy Spirit and springs from a passionate heart can rock the world. Caring relationships and the truth of God's word is a powerful combination. Let's toss aside the mechanical and work toward the vital!

"But you will receive power when the Holy Spirit has come upon you, and you will be my witnesses in Jerusalem and in all Judea and Samaria, and to the end of the earth" (Acts 1:8).

CREPE MYRTLE

ONE DAY, I ENTERED OUR upstairs TV room and was startled by bright, crepe myrtle blossoms peeking in from the window. I peered up at the tree and realized that it towered several feet above the roof of our house. Cheryl, an art director who was also our friend, brought that small bush over for a photo shoot shortly after our home was built. Now, I realized with a jolt, Cheryl had been dead for over twenty years, yet the little bush lived on. The bush's startling height and ability to produce two colors of flowers seems an appropriate tribute to our incredibly creative friend.

Cheryl never did anything halfway. She was a passionate, talented artist. When she began to imagine a photo for the magazine she produced, nothing seemed too hard. And much to the dismay of her staff, when Cheryl was at work, the element of time disappeared. This creative genius would arrive at four o'clock in the afternoon for a photo shoot that was supposed to begin at nine in the morning. Her creative mind was still gathering, planning, creating and she just wasn't ready at nine o'clock. She could easily work until two o'clock in the morning and never think about sleep. She was right smack dab in the deep, deep middle of the artistic zone.

I don't know, of course, but maybe heaven will be like that too. Maybe we will be so absorbed in the beauty and joy and love of God that everything else falls away. I suspect that nothing will matter except what really does matter. And that, of course, is the glory of God and the incredible glow of His love.

Everything that we have ever seen or experienced in our lives on earth has a beginning and an end. Our human brains cannot fully imagine the eternal, but as believers, we know that heaven is our hope and that time will not exist. I believe that we will be fully engaged in experiencing the full beauty of God. I believe that we will experience love so rich and so deep that our hearts float with pure and magnificent joy. Nothing will weigh us down. Thank you, God, for this hope! Thank you, God, for heaven!

> "And the city has no need of sun or moon, for the glory
> of God illuminates the city, and the Lamb is its light"
> (Revelation 21:23).

MELINDA ROGERS

NOTHING SPECIAL

W HEN I WAS AROUND TWELVE years old, my mother bought a photo album and asked me to fill it with our latest family photos. I was delighted and especially excited because the album had a place beside each photo slot to write a caption.

I efficiently wrote notes such as, "Melinda's twelfth birthday" or "Melinda's piano recital." Because my brother was four and very cute, my parents took a lot of random photos of him for no special occasion. So, in a way that made perfect sense to me, I wrote on these types of photos, "Jay, nothing special."

A few years later, my brother viewed the album and took great offense. The captions I had written about myself are now all marked out. If you look at the album today, you will see that beside each of the marked-out words, written in a childish hand, are the words, "Melinda, nothing special."

My brother misunderstood and took immediate action. Although his actions as a young child are hilarious, acting without understanding can be anything but funny as an adult. Haven't we all done it? We hear something that someone supposedly said about us or our families, and we speak out in anger or find a way to retaliate by talking to others about the ones who upset us. We forget to pause. We forget to pray.

As believers, we are something special, but we act like nothing special when we forget to invite God into all our difficult situations. I learned from friends I really admire that in difficult, anger-provoking moments, I should pray first and speak second. Often, we only have time to say, "God, help me," but if we call on Him—even with those few, short words—He will.

I am grateful that we can call on Him! In our conflicts and in our times of peace, He makes all the difference.

"Morning, noon and night I cry out in my distress, and the Lord hears my voice" (Psalm 55:17–19).

ERNIE

$\mathcal{E}$RNIE, A TALL MAN WITH a friendly smile, was at our home for several days restoring our cast-iron tub. He sauntered by as I worked on a lesson plan for a world-view class, and we struck up a conversation.

"Worldview, huh?" he said thoughtfully. "Have you ever been camping?"

"Yes," I said. "I loved it!"

"Weren't you so excited to go?"

"Yes," I said.

"But when the time came, weren't you ready to go home?" "Yes," I admitted. "Very ready!"

He nodded knowingly.

"Are you using that as an analogy about your worldview?" I asked. "That's brilliant!"

I understood what Ernie was telling me: camping can be great fun! We arrive full of energy and excitement and are thrilled by campfire cooking and sleeping in a tent. But after a day or so, the strain of the rugged life, the damp sleeping bags, and the smell of unshowered bodies all weigh us down. We look forward to the place where warm baths, clean sheets, and microwave ovens welcome us home.

Life on earth can easily become our all. We grasp onto the thrills, pleasures, and fun, but we are just as often weighed down by the work, strain, and stress. At the end of the day, our heavenly home is a place of joy and peace that our minds cannot even imagine. If Jesus is our Savior, we understand that life on earth is just a time of camping out. Our real home, our home with no tears or fears or sadness, is in heaven. Hallelujah! I am grateful for the time that God has given me here on earth, but I look forward to going home!

"But, we are citizens of heaven, where the Lord Jesus Christ lives. And we are eagerly waiting for him to return as Savior" (Philippians 3:20).

ROUND ABOUT

SOMETIMES LIFE IMITATES ART, AND sometimes it imitates a Chevy Chase movie. Ours did the latter when we visited San Antonio years ago. All we wanted was a nice, simple vacation. Who doesn't? But then again, how often are vacations truly simple? It seems to me that when you travel, you need to pack lots of underwear, socks, and a giant tank of "sense of humor." If you don't, oh boy, you might be in lots of trouble!

As soon as we left for our San Antonio trip that year, Truitt became nauseous. He stayed in the car while the kids and I visited the beautiful caverns we had planned to see along the way. Surely, we thought, he will be feeling better by the time we reach San Antonio. But no, he did not.

Truitt normally drove and was used to navigating unfamiliar cities. I, on the other hand, was much less experienced, but had cheerfully taken on the role of driver. However, my brave sense of cheer and goodwill began to morph into a sense of overwhelmed mortification as I tried to find the exit to our hotel during five o'clock traffic. Somehow, I had found myself on a loop where everyone around me was whizzing by. I could see our hotel in the group of buildings inside the loop, but I could not find the exit to get to it.

The first time around, I said, "Look, kids, there's our hotel. Doesn't it look nice?" The second time around, I said, "Look kids, there's our hotel. I sure wish I could find the exit." The third time around, I said, "Look, kids, the exit has to be around here somewhere!" The fourth time around, I said, "Help me, Jesus!" and we finally found our way. Some experiences in life remind me of that terrible day on the roundabout. Sometimes we get stuck in destructive patterns, or those we love constantly repeat the same mistakes and reap the same rotten consequences. We try and try to fix things, but nothing works.

Sometimes, we just need to cry out to our Savior with the simple, heartfelt words, "Help me, Jesus!" He hears. He loves you. He will help in the way that is best. You may have to wait. You may have to learn. You may have to hold on with faith that you can barely feel. But cry out! Hold on. He cares.

"I cry out to God Most High, to God who will fulfill his purpose for me" (Psalm 57:2).

FROM THE SUN

CLARKE, EMILY, AND I HAD just finished up a few fun days in Fredericksburg with my friend Carla. If you live in Texas, it is almost a given that you love the Hill Country with its rolling hills, abundant trees, wildlife, and quaint places to eat and shop. On our way back home, we decided to stop at McDonalds in Georgetown for a quick lunch. We were happily munching on hamburgers and carrying on a lively conversation when a young woman approached our table.

"Hi," she said. "I'm from the sun and I would like to ask you a few questions." From the sun? *Oh, brother*, I thought. *She must be from a cult. She wants to see if she can convert us to her strange beliefs about everyone originating from the sun.* Amazingly, Carla seemed to have reached the same conclusion. We gave each other a knowing glance, and I told the woman that we preferred not to talk.

Then I noticed something. The woman had moved to the next table, and I heard her asking the children how they felt about going back to school.

"This will make an interesting article for the paper," the mother said. Oh. The young woman was from a *newspaper* called *The Sun*.

I sought the reporter out, explained our erroneous assumption, and apologized. She ended up writing about our misunderstanding in her newspaper column that week. Boy, can we mess up when we assume things!

Unfortunately, many of us assume erroneous things about people on a regular basis. I have found myself assuming that someone is not a Christian because he or she goes to a different church. I can also make a lot of assumptions based on someone's hair and personal style. I'm glad that Jesus didn't do that. Jesus just loved, plain and simple. He approached people from many different walks of life and loved them all. I came to an important conclusion in those few eye-opening moments in Georgetown. I realized that even if the woman had been from a cult, I should have invited her to sit down with us, gotten to know her, and told her about Jesus.

I let my assumptions and desire to face inward to those I already know to get the in the way. Yet, I learned something that day. I hope I learned a little bit more about how to love like Jesus.

> "The Word gave life to everything that was created, And his life brought life to everyone" (John 1:4d).

BARRY

B ARRY MCGUIRE IS AN AMERICAN singer-songwriter, best known for his hit song "Eve of Destruction" in the 1960s. He was well-known to the kids of my generation and was considered a music icon. And one day, when I was sixteen years old, he rang my doorbell. I opened the door and, after I realized who was standing there, the door wasn't the only thing open. My mouth gaped as I tried to take it all in. Barry McGuire was at my door. *Barry McGuire.*

In retrospect, I wish I had engaged him in conversation. Instead, he invited me to a Christian concert that was being held at the TCU theatre that evening. I eagerly took the brochure he handed me and promised him that I would come. Barry McGuire was at my door. Barry McGuire was a Christian. I was astounded.

In later years, I was able to read his bio online, and I realized that he had just become a Christian when he came to my home. He was just beginning his journey as a pioneer in contemporary Christian music. Because Jesus had transformed his life, Barry McGuire, who could be living the highlife in any city in the world, knocked on the door of my suburban home in Fort Worth, Texas. He glowed with an enthusiasm that was contagious.

After his encounter with Christ, the glamorous life that the world promotes must had suddenly looked very dull. God took Barry in a different direction, and he made an amazing impact on Christian music. He brought the luring sounds of '60s rock and folk music to the Christian music scene. His music makes an impact to this day. How inspiring it is to see someone turn away from the world and face Christ with open arms. Help me, God, to do the same. I am yours.

> "Jesus replied, "You must love the Lord your God with all your heart, all your soul, and all your mind. This is the first and greatest commandment" (Matthew 22:37).

HOW MANY JOBS?

*W*HEN OUR GRANDSON ADRIAN WAS five, he began to do some important research for his future. "How many jobs can you have when you grow up?" he asked his mother.

"That really depends," she told him. "What jobs are you wanting?"

"Well," he told her confidently, "I want to go into space in the morning. Then I want to come back from space in the afternoon and be a chef. Then, when it is evening, I want to be a fireman. When it is night, I will be a policeman."

Ah! The fervor of youth! As adults, we sometimes find it hard to get up each morning to face one job, not to mention four! When we are children, anything seems possible. Dreaming of a bright and fabulous tomorrow is as natural as eating a cookie or playing outside. It is simply what children do. Yet, as we age, some of our difficult experiences create doubt, fear, and exhaustion that sit like bubble-bursting weights on our fragile dreams.

None of us, of course, could work simultaneously as an astronaut, chef, police officer, and fire fighter. But what dreams are we cramming under the sofa cushions because we are scared or tired? Maybe we should all raise our hands up to God and ask him to remove those heavy weights of doubt. Maybe we should ask God to show us how to dream and how our dreams might further His kingdom.

Are you afraid to do that? Ask Him to help you be unafraid. Ask Him to show you where to go and how to get there. Ah! The fervor of believers!

> "For I can do everything through Christ who gives me strength" (Philippians 4:13).

SNAKE STORY

*A*S CHILDREN, WE OFTEN VISITED my aunt Fern, who lived in east Texas. I loved her house because it was very large and old and had colorful stained glass surrounding the oversized front door. On one of our visits, I was playing in her side yard when I dropped a box of toy gun caps onto the thick green grass. I bent over to pick them up when I heard a distinctive rattling sound. Turning around just in time, I saw a rattlesnake with his mouth open, headed right toward my ankle.

Within a split second, my ankle and the rest of me were sprinting toward to house. The snake just missed his target! I told my mom and my aunt what had happened, and they downplayed my report. "Oh, you probably just saw a lizard," they assured me. Fortunately, my aunt went out to double-check and ended up running for the hoe. The snake was dead within minutes.

Now, this story isn't the greatest adventure story of all time, but to ten-year-old me, it certainly was. I couldn't wait to get home and tell of my friends about my incredible near-death (or at least near-injury) experience. I told the story over and over with great satisfaction as my friends gasped in amazement. The scare was real, but the story-telling rights were worth it!

I think of that sometimes when I am going through a difficult situation. I no longer aim to impress my friends with my near-death experiences, but I *do* want to encourage others. Fortunately, as believers, our rough times can often be redeemed for good in others' lives when we share how God sustained us through the dark times. My friend Nicole was certainly a bright-and-shining star in my life when my daughter-in-law was diagnosed with breast cancer. Beautiful, healthy, happy Nicole had been through the same thing and was still going strong. She encouraged our whole family with her story of God's help and strength.

Let's pray that our stories, both the good ones and the hard ones, can be used for good to further God's kingdom. I am glad that our stories are written by the king!

"He comforts us in all our troubles so that we can comfort others. When they are troubled, we will be able to give them the same comfort God has given us" (2 Corinthians 1:4).

CRUTCH

WHEN I WAS IN THE fourth grade, I injured my ankle. My mom tended to it and told me that it would be better in time. My dad, on the other hand, decided to take things a step further. In a burst of ingenuity, he fashioned for me a homemade crutch from a broom's handle and a rubber cap. It felt like Christmas! Yes, I was that pitiful.

I was thrilled to have a prop that would cause others to notice me and to show sympathy, except, it didn't really work out that way.

"What's that?" my dubious friends asked as they noticed my broomstick crutch.

"I hurt my foot," I replied. "Hmmm," they answered.

By the end of the day, the crutch was tossed aside, and I hobbled around without my once-adored broomstick. For some reason, the "day of the crutch" has stuck with me through the years. The story is a reminder of the need that we humans have for attention and concern. My need, of course, was childish and played out in a childish way, but we all want to be noticed and cared for.

Jesus was the absolute best at noticing and caring. He noticed the sick, the oppressed, and the weak. He looked them in the eyes, saw them for who they were, and met their needs. I want to focus less on my own need for attention and to be like Jesus. Lord, give me opportunities to turn my attention to others and to show them your love and care.

> "Love each other with genuine affection and take delight in honoring each other" (Romans 12:10).

GOVERNMENT OFFICE

*T*HE DAY WAS CLOUDY AND unseasonably cool for an August morning in Texas. I had an unexpected caregiver for my mom, and I had several errands to run while the running was good. I had two fun shopping errands and one errand I dreaded—very much. Ugh. I needed to go to the country clerk's office to renew my mom's parking placard for the disabled. *I would rather have a tooth filled*, I thought as I drove into the parking lot. Past experiences at government offices filled me with dread.

I began the necessary motivating self-talk. "Yes, you read what you needed to do to renew the placard online, but the rules may have changed. There is a good chance you won't get the renewal. You will probably have to wait forever, but it is OK. Remember, no one is dying either way. It is all OK."

Imagine my shock when I walked into the office and several smiling faces whipped around to greet me and say hello. "How may I help you today?" asked one smiling young woman.

I told her what I needed and handed her my form. "We will get those for you right away," she told me cheerfully.

Not being one to hold back any though that pops into my head, I said, "You sure are nice!" She just smiled and thanked me for the compliment.

While she was getting my placards, I heard a nearby clerk telling a funny story. She was laughing so hard that she could barely get the words out. Everyone in the office was smiling.

Man, I thought, *I want to work here. I wonder if they have any part time jobs.* Huh? Melinda Rogers contemplating a job in a government office for even one second. This place was not what I expected!

As I thought about the lift to my spirit that came because of the unexpected kindness, I wondered how I could give unexpected kindness to others. What about the man or woman on the other end of a sales call? What about the police officers giving me a ticket? How could I brighten others' days with the love I have because Jesus loves me? Jesus certainly surprised people with kindness. He cared. He healed. He delivered people from demons. He didn't care about their positions or consider anyone unworthy of His love.

OK, that's a lot of love lessons gleaned from a simple visit to the county clerk's office. But, hey, Jesus teaches us how to live our lives in many unexpected ways. He teaches us to love.

> "Instead, by kind to each other, tenderhearted, forgiving one another, just as God through Christ has forgiven you" (Ephesians 4:32).

SUZY SMART

I WAS ABSOLUTELY MESMERIZED BY THE commercial on our small black-and-white television. Suzy Smart. I was five years old, and Suzy Smart appeared to be the answer to my little girl prayers. She was a doll, but not just any doll. She was a doll that could jump right out of the box, play with you, and become your very best friend. That is exactly how this amazing doll was portrayed in the advertisement, and I believed it!

I believed that if I could receive a Susy Smart doll for Christmas, my world would never be the same. I was the only child at the time, and the thought of a playful little sister seemed like a dream come true. But my dreams were turned to stark reality when I opened the Susy Smart box on Christmas morning. Susy did *not* jump out of the box and ask to play with me. In fact, the hard plastic girl just sat there and stared. My parents encouraged me to pull her string, but Suzy would only speak in a disheartening monotone. With each pull, she said, "My name is Suzy Smart. C-A-T spells cat; one plus one equals two."

Suzy was a major disappointment.

I learned at an early age that advertising can be false. What can be sold to us as bright and shiny can really be dull and useless. Isn't that true of so many things that the world constantly tries to sell us? If you are beautiful and thin, you will be happy! If you have plenty of money, your joy will never end. If you reach your career goals, you will be admired by all who know you. That type of false advertising bombards us daily.

We are happiest when we keep our hearts wide open to being the best we can be, but not for our glory. We are happiest when we let the Holy Spirit guide us into lives of love for God and others, humility, integrity, and passion for the gospel of Jesus Christ. The world preaches lies. God's word, our incredible instruction book for life, never lets us down.

> **"So be careful how you live. Don't live like fools, but like those who are wise.** Make the most of every opportunity in these evil days. Don't act thoughtlessly but understand what the Lord wants you to do" (Ephesians 5:15–17).

IN THE GAME

*E*VEN THOUGH OUR SON, CLARKE, seemed to be born with an aversion to any type of jacket, I insisted on buying him a warm coat before he left for college. The coat stayed in the trunk of his car for four years. Oh well. However, a little stocking stuffer that we purchased for Clarke during his college years became important and surprisingly useful. The keychain was probably a last-minute shopping whim, but the attached miniature Monopoly game seemed the perfect little gift for our game-loving son.

Little did we know how important they keychain would be to Clarke and his friend Stephen. The two college friends were traveling across the flatlands of west Texas on their way to Colorado when Stephen's car began to fail. Something was terribly wrong. Before they knew it, the two travelers were sitting in a dusty garage hearing terrible news from the mechanic. The car could not be repaired, there was no cell service, and there was no town within walking distance. They were stranded.

Like all good prisoners, Stephen was allowed one phone call. The gas station owners handed him their phone, and he called his parents, who said that they would be there as soon as they could. "As soon as they could" would be about five hours. After a few minutes of pondering the long, boring day before them, Clarke suddenly remembered something. He had the tiny Monopoly game on his keychain.

Before boredom and disappointment could take hold, the boys found themselves engrossed in a full-fledged, robust round of one of their favorite games. The game came with tiny dice and tiny tokens. There was no play money or cards, but Clarke was able to remember each detail of the cards and devise a dice-rolling system that indicated which "card" you "drew.. Money was tallied on a piece of paper. Playing on the tiny board with the creative work-arounds added extra humor to the once-grim situation. They played for hours and hours.

That tiny board helped Clarke and Stephen make it through a time of disappointment and helplessness. Sometimes, the smallest of things can be of the most help.

Jesus once spoke to his disciples about something incredibly small. He told them that if they had faith the size of a tiny mustard seed that they could move mountains. That teaching comes to me when I am feeling disappointed or helpless. Nothing is impossible for God if we trust Him. While we wait, with even the tiniest sliver of faith, we can make it through with hope.

"I tell you the truth, if you had faith even as small as a mustard seed, you could say to this mountain, 'Move from here to there,' and it would move. Nothing would be impossible" (Matthew 17:20).

AJAX CAKE

IF THERE IS SUCH A thing as a girl scout hall of fame, I will not be nominated. Truth be told, I joined the Girl Scouts only because there was not a Camp Fire Girl group established for my grade. The Camp Fire Girls had much, much prettier uniforms, and earning colorful beads seemed a lot more exciting than sewing on patches.

But despite the drab green uniforms, I bravely signed up and joined my friends in the Girl Scouts. My attitude improved quite a bit when my mother gave me a lovely Girl Scout purse for my eleventh birthday. *Maybe,* I thought, *I can make this green look work for me.*

Yes, you might just say that my priorities were not exactly those of the esteemed Juliet Lowe. But as it happened, I did learn a lot in Girl Scouts and experienced many fun days with my troop. However, one of my days at Girl Scout Day Camp was not fun at all. The day started poorly because I could never get the hang of making those camp requisite lanyards. *Maybe,* I thought, *I will feel better when it is time for lunch.*

At mealtime, we mixed up a cake batter and poured it into a large Dutch oven. "If you know the trick," our counselor proudly told us, "You can cook anything over a fire, even a cake!"

We ate our lunch and looked forward to the cake, but we shouldn't have. After just one bite, we could taste Ajax cleanser. Someone had cleaned out the Dutch oven but had failed to rinse it well. After a few seconds, we were gagging and throwing our slices of cake into the trash can. That action was another "shouldn't have."

Our counselor was *not* having it. "You girls do not waste food! Get those slices out of the trash right now and eat them," she told us.

Scared to disobey the fearsome woman, we obeyed. Yes, we ate Ajax-flavored cake from the trash can. The drab Girl Scout uniforms were one thing, but this … I remembered the Ajax cake recently when I was harsh with a loved one. I had let some bitterness and anger taint my spirit. Sweetness and bitterness mix like an Ajax cake. Bitterness always seems to win out over sweetness and taints our relationships. I asked the Lord right then to forgive me and to cleanse the "Ajax" out of my spirit. I want to be a vessel that grows sweeter not more bitter. I want to be kind, not rude. Reflecting Christ cannot be accomplished with a bitter spirit. I am grateful that the Lord teaches all of us, even those of us with poor priorities and bad lanyard making skills.

> **"Get rid of all bitterness, rage, anger, harsh words, and slander, as well as all** types of evil behavior. Instead, be kind to each other, tenderhearted, forgiving one another, just as God through Christ has forgiven you" (Ephesians 4:31–32).

FREE CHURCH

MOST PEOPLE DON'T KNOW THIS about me, but at the age of fifteen, I started a church. Incredible, isn't it? The church may have lasted only one hour and been ended by an angry police officer, but I did start a church. It was 1971, and my young mind was filled with all kinds of vague ideas about freedom and getting away from the "establishment." I had listened to too many rock songs and had not spent enough time studying God's word. But, on the positive side, I did love the Lord and wanted to start something new for Him.

So, in my youthful naivety, I called my group of friends and asked them to meet downtown at the park for free church. I confess, I did not really know what a free church was, but I had heard the term somewhere and thought it sounded cool. A few of the guys arrived with their guitars, and we sang a song or two. Then, I suddenly realized that being "free" and not having a plan could be a little awkward. What were we to do next?

I'm not sure whose idea it was, but in our desire to do something besides just sit there trying to figure out free church, we found ourselves inside the park's concrete shelter, writing scripture on the walls. Yes, we were defacing public property with scripture. We weren't fulfilling the great commission; we were committing a crime! So, as you have guessed by now, a police officer came along and angrily told us to clean up the walls. We waited until he left and then rushed to our cars and skedaddled right back to our suburban homes nestled in the heart of the "establishment."

Suddenly, the "establishment" looked very attractive! We were young and naïve, but the whole sordid story is a picture of moving ahead in ministry with our own ideas, our own motives, and without the leadership of God. As we look for ways to serve the Lord and pray for our church homes, let's also pray to be led by the Spirit and directed by God's word. Let's pray to be servants who follow God's agenda and not our own. Surrendering to His leading creates true freedom!

"Your word is a lamp to guide my feet and a light for my path" (Psalm 119:105).

COOKBOOK

I DON'T KNOW ABOUT YOU, BUT my favorite way to find new recipes is to scour church cookbooks. When you think about it, every single recipe in the book is someone's very favorite. I can't think of a recipe I have tried from a church cookbook that wasn't tasty. Over the years, I have collected a few of these remarkable cookbooks from all over the country. Yet, my favorite is one that I inherited from my mother-in-law.

Yes, the recipes in the book are good. Yes, the 1970s graphics are fun. But the best things about this cookbook are the laughs it brings. My mother-in-law was a sweet, laughing, enthusiastic, gushing southern woman. Yet, evidently, when she got mad—watch out. If she got mad at you, you might just find your name in her church cookbook marked out with pen and then painted over with Wite-Out. I don't know what happened, but there was a certain group of ladies who my mother-in-law once shopped and lunched with who *all* had their names unceremoniously removed from her cookbook. That was "unfriending," 1970s church-ladies style!

The case of the marked-out cookbook names reminds me that even the happiest of people with the sweetest of hearts can let anger destroy relationships. Every couple who has ever gone to premarital counseling has been told that you must work to maintain love and harmony in the home. I think that we sometimes forget that when it comes to friends. Let's face it: there is not one perfect friend in the whole world. None of us are perfect. Just as we must forgive and communicate well in marriage, we must do the same thing in friendships. Sometimes friends hurt us. Sometimes friends provoke us. Sometimes friends let us down. Only Jesus is the perfect friend.

When friends wound you, pray. Ask God to help you forgive. Remember that forgiveness is almost always a process. If you find that you cannot forget, pray for wisdom and humility, and then talk to your friend with an open heart. No need to whip out the Wite-Out and delete every friend who has made you mad!

"So, if you are presenting a sacrifice at the alter in the Temple and your suddenly remember that someone has something against you, leave your sacrifice there at the altar. Go and be reconciled to that person. Then come and offer your sacrifice to God" (Matthew 5:23–24).

GORILLA

I WAS GOING ABOUT MY USUAL day at home when I heard the front door crash open. I rushed into the living room just in time to see Truitt tossing off his shirt and pants. Before I could even ask him about his strange behavior, he was in the shower making good use of soap and hot water.

It was then that I noticed the smell. The clothes on the living room floor were covered in something rancid. What in the world?

"Truitt," I demanded to my still showering husband, "what happened?"

"You know that photography job I had today at the zoo?"

"Yes."

"Well, it was going great for a while. One of the zoo employees and I went into the barrier area in front of the gorilla cage so I could get a close-up shot. Next thing I knew the employee was shouting, 'Watch out! He's going to throw it!' I didn't know what to think. It seemed to me that the gorilla was just playing with something in his hands. Then splat. He hit me with his smelly gift. Do I look like a human toilet?"

We will never forget that day. That gorilla will live in the Rogers' stinky memories hall of shame forever!

I sometimes think of that gorilla when life hurls unexpected stink bombs. Those happen more often than we would like, don't they? I think one of the hardest unexpected bombs in life are the bombs of hurt. You will feel like you are doing a great job at work, but your boss promotes someone else with less experience. You find out that a friend has said unkind things about you behind your back. Your spouse chooses to go camping with his or her friends on your anniversary weekend. Your son or daughter makes it clear that he or she does not want to spend time with you. Many of us have a memory list of hurts hidden deep within.

If you are a parent, then you have even more opportunities to experience hurt. Anytime someone hurts your child, I believe that it hurts you more. Yep. Sometimes the stink bombs just come hurling and hurting out of left field. We are left shocked and aching. We want to escape the pain, but we can't simply jump into the shower and wash off the smell. If we are wise, we go first to our loving Father with our hurts. We pour our hearts out. We ask for wisdom. And then we wait.

Hurt takes time to heal, and sometimes, it never heals completely. But our loving Father cares. He will bind our wounds and use our pain for good. If we take our hurts to our Father, He will teach us about joy that supersedes circumstance and will keep our hurts from forming a hard shell of bitterness. Life can stink; that's a cold fact. But when we turn to Him, we smell nothing but a sweet aroma.

> "Yet, I am confident I will see the Lord's goodness while I am here in the land of the living. Wait patiently for the Lord. Be brave and courageous. Yes, wait patiently for the Lord" (Psalm 27:13–14).

POSTERS

*Y*OU MAY NOT KNOW THIS about me, but I played a very important role in ending the war in Vietnam. Yes, sir. I placed a bumper sticker that said, "Who is going to arrest war for disturbing the peace?" in my bedroom, wore a love-and-peace dove necklace, and sang along with all the peace -promoting songs on the radio. I am pretty sure that these self-sacrificing efforts made a big difference in influencing President Nixon to withdraw the troops. I am kidding, of course. My efforts did nothing but disturb my parents and give me a misdirected sense of self-satisfaction.

Ironically, it was my flag-loving, army veteran father who taught me a real lesson about peace. He did not like the antiwar and rock star posters that decorated my bedroom as a teenager. But, unlike many parents of my peers, he didn't complain. He never pointed out how disturbing and wrong they were. He never puffed up with offense and finger-pointing judgement. Instead, I came home one day and discovered that my dad had placed his own poster up in my parents' bedroom across the hall from mine. I might have been a very cool, wannabe hippie, but I could not help myself. I had to laugh. There, on my parents' beige walls, was a large, glossy poster of John Wayne in front of an American flag. The all-American star of war and cowboy movies grinned at me from his paper home as if to say, "See? I'm the real deal. Your rock stars are nothing."

My dad didn't say a word, but he had made a bold statement. First Corinthians 15:49 tells us that, as believers, we are to reflect our heavenly Father. I think my earthly father gave me a living example of how to do that in situations that involve different viewpoints on social or political situations. He didn't condemn. He didn't finger-point. He simply reflected what he believed, calmly explained his viewpoint when asked, and reflected the love of our heavenly Father. When I am tempted to post a self-satisfying comment on social media, I remember my pitiful peace efforts of 1971. They did nothing. We cannot further God's kingdom with bumper stickers or media posts. We will, however, make a difference in this world as believers if we reflect the love and peace of our heavenly Father. Stand firm in the truth of God's word and stand firm in love. Love and peace. Did I understand in 1971, that God was the author of them both?

> **"Peace be with you, dear brothers and sisters, and may God the Father and the Lord Jesus Christ give you love with faithfulness"** (Ephesians 6:23).

JOHN DEERE

TRUITT IS A WARRIOR OF the bravest, most adventurous kind when he drives his John Deere tractor. He is never happier than when he is riding command over the fields and shaping the rebellious, weed-sprouting land into shape. Because he has absolutely no fear, my husband seldom remains unscathed. Despite his ever-present hat, Truitt's head has endured many a scratch and sunburn from low-hanging branches and the Texas sun. Yet, because he's a warrior with a tractor-sized passion, he carries on. You can find him on his John Deere almost every week in the summer. And believe me, you will find him with a smile on his face.

But even the bravest of warriors can be blindsided. One day, I was inside while Truitt mowed. Suddenly, there was a loud noise, and the house seemed to shake in its boots. Earthquake, I wondered? No. No earthquake.

That day, our yard was unwatered, unnourished, and no longer green. Because of this sad situation, a cloud of dust kicked up around Truitt's tractor as he mowed. The dust blinded him, and he didn't see the corner of the house. We can make the same mistake in our walks with God. We tell ourselves that we are too busy to dig into God's word or to spend time with the Lord in prayer. Like my pitiful summer yard, we can easily become unwatered and unnourished. We can become blinded by the dust that life throws into our eyes and easily hit a wall.

Fortunately, neither Truitt nor the house suffered major damage from the great tractor crash of 2019. Hitting a spiritual wall and trying to live life without God can have much worse consequences. Stay in God's Word. Stay in prayer. Stay away from those walls!

> "When the ground soaks up the falling rain and bears a good crop for the farmer, it has God's blessing. But if a field bears thorns and thistles, it is useless" (Ephesians 6:7–8a).

FLOOD PLAN

*W*HEN MY FRIENDS AND I were teens, we would gobble down tacos and burgers at lunch and talk about boys. When we were young adults, we would sit over salads to discuss husbands, jobs, and the unpredictable world of raising kids. Later, the topics turned to empty nests, career moves, and travel. Then I realized one fall day when I was in my sixties that my friends and I had reached a new level of conversation.

Kathy and I had barely settled into our chairs at the tearoom when Margaret arrived and burst out with her news.

"John and I bought our burial plots," she said.

"Oh," I stated encouragingly. "That's good! Those are expensive."

"Oh no," Margaret enthused. "Our plots are in the floodplain. We got them for a real bargain!".

"That's great!" We laughed.

Suddenly, Margaret got a serious look on her face and asked an important favor. "So, if we go before you guys and it rains really hard, will you make sure that we don't float away?"

For the rest of the day, I kept picturing Kathy and me with raincoats and umbrellas running after the Martins' caskets, and I could *not* stop laughing. Time does not stop. Each of us age with every passing second. Yet, as believers, we can face aging with courage. We can laugh about chasing caskets because we know that we will be with our Father as soon as we take our last breaths. Oh, the difference the hope of heaven makes! Thank you, Lord!

> "And now, dear brothers and sisters, we want you to know what will happen to the believers who have died so you will not grieve like people who have no hope" (1 Thessalonians 4:13).

MOURNING GLORIES

I STEPPED OUT ONTO MY FRONT porch and observed some small vines making their way around the posts. Last year at this time, I lamented, giant blooms covered the railing in a glorious profusion of purples and blues. This year, the morning glory vines appeared weak, yellowed, and tired. They had not produced a single bloom.

How sad, I thought. *What a disappointing year.* Then I saw motion and heard buzzing. Just to the right of the sad morning glory vines, butterflies and bees hovered around a glorious stand of giant zinnias. Even though it was already October, the beautiful array of flowers kept producing amazing colors that seemed to wave happily in the autumn breeze.

Oh, brother, I chastised myself. *You focused on the sad vines and forgot to be grateful for the zinnias.*

Life changes. Some people leave us. Jobs go away. Health issues surprise us. It is right to be sad. It is good to mourn. But if we focus only on the difficult things, we fail to see the blessings that are often in plain view.

When you are sad, list ten things for which you are grateful. It is absolutely astounding how much this exercise lifts the spirits. If you are still struggling, list twenty! Share your list with a friend or someone in your family. The joy doubles! Give your hurts and your sadness to the Lord. Hand your pain over to your Father who loves you. Jesus knew hurt. Jesus knew pain. He knew these things as part of the great plan of salvation that our loving Father put in the place. Put this amazing sacrifice of Jesus right at the top of your gratitude list!

> "Throw off your sinful nature and your former way of life, which is corrupted by lust and deception. Instead, let the Spirit renew your thoughts and attitudes" (Ephesians 4:22–23).

UFOS

*W*E WERE ON A MISSION. My friend Susan and I, two imaginative sixth graders, had absolutely no doubt that we could find evidence that would astound the world. For reasons I can no longer remember, we were certain that UFOs had visited our town and had landed in the wooded area behind our elementary school. We spent several warm Saturdays combing the area and gathering proof. Any small piece of metal, plastic, or rubber we discovered brought us great delight. "Look!" we would shout. "This probably fell off one of the spaceships!" Even with all these amazing finds, we were never able to prove our theory of local alien visitations. Why the adults in our lives failed to listen to our theories despite our big bag of "evidence" is beyond me. Shockingly, we never became famous for our incredible discoveries.

Looking back on these adventures with Susan makes me laugh. We obviously were trying to make our evidence fit our narrative. We wanted to believe in local UFOs, so anything we found "proved" their existence. Sadly, we sometimes keep up this poor habit as adults. We find a narrative that appeals to us, and we try our best to prove that it is right and good. "I know what God says about sex, but …" "I know what the Bible says about honesty, but …" "I know what the pastor said last week about loving others, but …" We have all done it. We have heard the truth and tried to worm our way around it by making excuses and finding fake evidence that counters what we know is right.

Lies are thrown at us each day. It is easy to fall for them. Our greatest defense against them is the truth. Where do we find the truth? God's word, of course. Stay there. Pray there. God's word is powerful, and its narrative leads us straight to God. Stay there. Pray there. What a wonderful place to be.

> "How can a young person stay pure? By obeying your word" (Psalm 119:9).

DROP IN

ONE BRIGHT SATURDAY MORNING WHEN the kids were small, I lingered longer than usual in my robe and did some baking. Truitt was in the living room testing out his new stereo system, and the kids ran back and forth between the two of us. They danced to the music with Truitt and scooped up bits of chocolate from my baking project. In a word, we were living in a chocolate, rock and roll, wild bit of chaotic fun. Suddenly above the sounds of the rock music, I heard a faint ringing noise. Could that be the doorbell?

"Oh no," I whispered as I looked down at my chocolate-covered robe and envisioned the state of my uncombed hair. The kids came running into the kitchen with big chocolate-mouth smiles, telling me that Mamaw and Grandpa had dropped by.

It got worse. Not only had Truitt's mom and dad dropped by, but they had brought Truitt's great aunt Pauline and a group of distant cousins from California to see our house. Yes, they brought visitors by for a home tour without calling in advance. I plastered on a smile and did my best to be a good hostess, yet inside, I was mortified with embarrassment.

Now, I look back at the day with a totally different perspective. I am grateful that our little family had moments of unbridled and totally undignified fun. I'm glad that we shared moments with chocolate-smudged faces and food-stained robes. I'm glad that we danced to loud rock and roll music and laughed without a care. The state of our house doesn't matter; the state of our homelife is everything.

Jesus did not speak a word about keeping a tidy home. In fact, he asked us to stay away from earthly treasures and focus on heaven. So many things in society encourage us to focus on our own images, yet when we focus on Him, our images fade peacefully away.

> "Don't store up treasures here on earth, where moths eat them and rust destroys them, and where thieves break in and steal. Store your treasure in heaven, where moths and rust cannot destroy, and thieves do not break in and steal. Wherever your treasure is, there the desires of your heart will also be" (Matthew 6:19–21).

DUCKS

ONE SPRING, I LOST ALL rational thought. That is the only explanation I have for the fact that we ended up with a plastic swimming pool and a dozen baby ducks in the garage apartment behind our house. The kids, of course, were thrilled. The apartment, normally rented, was vacant, and the ducks, formerly housed in our backyard, had been attacked by a dog. So, what else could we do? We gave the ducks their own place.

Duck Tracy, Duck Van Dyke, and all the rest of gang were living the high life. Except that they weren't. The plastic swimming pool was a poor substitution for a lake or pond. The carpet was certainly not as sweet or soft as a meadow full of grass. The great little apartment was not the great outdoors. When the ducks were a little bigger, we finally regained our sanity and moved them to a pond in the country. They didn't hesitate for one second, and they flew. The apartment was not their real home.

I think of the ducks when I feel uncomfortable here on earth. As I get older, I realize more and more that the great song writer/singer Jim Reeves was right! "This world is not my home; I'm just passing through." Sometimes I truly feel like a duck in a plastic swimming pool, longing for my beautiful lake. That longing we sometimes have for heaven, I believe is from the Holy Spirit. Everything in us knows that this world is dark and that our true home will be filled with pure joy and light so bright that we cannot take it all in. In the meantime, I will swim peacefully in my plastic swimming pool full of hope for what is ahead. But, brothers and sisters, hold on to your hats because some wonderful day we will fly!

> "Yes, we are fully confident, and we would rather be away from these earthly bodies for then we will be at home with the Lord" (2 Corinthians 5:8).

WE DON'T TALK ABOUT IT

*W*HEN OUR GRANDSON HUSTON WAS a toddler, he spent Thursday mornings in a children's program at our church while his mom attended Bible study. Because she is a caring mom, Jennifer would often buckle Huston in his car seat and ask him several questions about his morning in class. Because boys, even baby ones, are not usually into answering those types of questions, Huston would consistently give very little response. But Jennifer persevered.

One morning, she buckled Huston in and asked the usual questions. Suddenly, with a furrowed brow and burst of bravado, Huston found his autonomous toddler voice and proclaimed loudly, "We don't talk about it nursery!" Now, when any of our family wants a break from talking about something, we say, "We don't talk about it (fill in the blank)."

I think about funny-little toddler Huston when pondering the art of conversation. Although his communication was clear, he had much to learn about the productive back-and-forth rhythm of human dialogue. We all have so much to learn about good conversation. When is it appropriate to ask questions? When is it a good idea to be silent? Colossians 4:6 says, "Let your conversation be gracious and attractive so that you will have the right responses for everyone." Our conversations can make or break our witness for reflection of Christ.

Our words are an extremely big deal! Most of us have a conversation tendency that, if not watched, can wreak havoc. My tendency is to ask five million questions about everything. Truitt has often said, "I don't recall what she said after that, or what he said before that. I think I need to start recording all my conversations so you will know the details!"

Some people I know have the opposite tendency. They are so busy spurting out every thought that enters their heads that they do not have time to ask anyone else anything. Others tend to have eyes that glass over while you are speaking, indicating that they couldn't care less what you have to say. Some people, of course, tend toward gossip or maliciousness. What is your tendency?

I have found that it was helpful to identify the tendency that trips me up and then pray for wisdom with my words. You might want to try praying for words of wisdom before you go to lunch with friends. Pray before that work meeting or dinner with the family. And if someone brings up a subject you don't want to discuss, remember, just say, "We don't talk about it (fill in the blank)." Just kidding!

"May the words of my mouth and the meditation of my heart be pleasing to you, O Lord, my rock and my redeemer" (Psalm 19:14).

BAD ROOM

*W*HEN EMILY LOOKS AT OUR photo albums and studies her childhood pictures, she often groans. "Why, Mom? Why? Why did you buy me hairbows and eyeglasses that were the size of Texas? They look ridiculous!" I have tried to convince her that giant glasses and bows were in style in the 1980s, but I am not sure that she has ever believed me.

Big glasses and big hairbows were just one of the over-the-top trends of the '80s. Home fashion was over the top as well. Victorian poufs and flowers and ribbons ran amuck through all the self-respecting 1980s Texas homes. And, believe me, I wanted to be part of the great amuck! With puffy Victorian dreams in mind, Truitt and I set out one weekend to redo our bedroom. We bought yards of burgundy fabric, lace, wood, and paint. I sat at the sewing machine making a comforter and curtains, while Truitt painted and made cornice boards.

The kids were young, but there were no fun outings or time spent playing outside together that weekend. We were on a mission. And as it turns out, a ridiculous mission at that. Truitt and I still shake our heads when we recall the late hour that Saturday night when all our new creations were in place. He looked at me. I looked at him. After our hard, tiring work, nothing in us wanted to admit it, but there was no denying it. Our room looked like a brothel. We laugh about it now, but that night, we wanted to cry. We ripped almost everything down and went to bed.

Unfortunately, I have spent a lot of time and money and effort on other projects that did not turn out well or that had no real value. Efforts in futility are, of course, simply a part of life. But wouldn't it be a shame if we got to the end of our lives and realized that almost everything we did was futile? To avoid that terrible situation, we need to constantly evaluate our priorities. We can do that by asking ourselves these questions: What are the things that God's word asks us to focus on? How is my life reflecting Christ? What difference am I making for God's kingdom and eternity?

The work you do for God doesn't have to be like a giant 1980s hairbow, but the simplest step toward imitating Christ can make a giant Texas-sized difference.

> "Never be lazy, but work hard and serve the Lord enthusiastically" (Romans 12:11).

FISH

I GOT OUT OF MY CAR and headed cheerfully toward to the pet store in search of fantail goldfish. I had recently lost some of the fish in my pond and was anxious to see what the store had in stock. Pulling into the parking lot at the same time as me was a young woman with braids in her hair. She walked just a few steps ahead of me and headed toward the fish department as well. Because she arrived a few seconds before me, the clerk asked if he could help her before acknowledging me.

"Yes," she said thoughtfully. "I need a few goldfish." She pointed to the thirty-nine-cent tank swarming with hundreds of fish.

"Ok," she said slowly. "For my first fish, I think I want that one in the corner with the white dot under its eye. Can you see it?"

Can this be real? I pondered to myself. *You are going to make that poor clerk sift through hundreds of fish that all look alike to find all the particular goldfish that you want?*

It was real. The goldfish selecting and scooping went on for quite some time. Did I feel patient? No. Did I feel love toward my fellow fish lover? No. On the other hand, was having to wait on the picky fish lady that big a deal? No. Was she doing anything malicious toward me? No. Could I possibly even laugh at the situation? Maybe.

When I finally headed toward the checkout desk with my fantails, guess who was in the line ahead of me? Guess who was holding up the line because she wanted to talk about her farm and her chickens and her everything? Of course, it was my braided-hair fish friend.

Did I feel patient? No. Did I ask for God's help to be patient? Yes. After praying, was I able to relax? Yes. Was this whole episode just a part of living on God's earth with our fellow humans? Yes. Could I be grateful that my life was so good that this small interruption felt so big? Yes. Ah. God, help me to see things in perspective. I can make little things big and big things little. I want to see the world as you do!

"Since you have been raised to new life with Christ, set your sights on the realities of heaven, where Christ sits in the place of honor at God's right hand. Think about the things of heaven, not the things of earth" (Colossians 3:1–2).

NEVER KNEW

*W*HEN THE KIDS WERE VERY small, I decided to run an ad in the local newspaper, seeking work as an in-home babysitter. We needed a little bit more monthly income, and I enjoyed children, so I ran the ad and prayed for the best. We received the best. When he was just three years old, Benjamin came into our home a few days each week and instantly became like part of our family. He and Clarke bonded over all kinds of little boy things like balloon fights and hot wheels races. And because he didn't have his own little sister, Ben enjoyed Emily's company as well.

Years later, after all three kids were adults, I heard a story from Clarke that astounded me. He told me that each day, when the much-loved *Transformers* cartoon show came on TV, that he would tell Ben to leave the room so that he could watch the show alone. Then, when the show ended, Clarke would call Ben back into the room and recount the whole episode to the appreciative Ben.

What? I never, ever, ever knew that. I had always considered myself a hands-on, highly involved, watchful mom. But evidently, this tradition went on for months and months. Clarke was not malicious in this TV-watching system. He enjoyed telling Ben the storyline each day, and Ben certainly never complained. But, of course, had I known of the situation, I would have stopped it immediately and allowed Ben to watch the show.

This revelation given to me about a situation from so long ago made me think about all the things we think we know that we really don't. We think we know why someone acts the way he or she does. We think we know everything about our families. We think we have a complete grasp on our pasts. We think we know what is best for our futures. We do not.

Our knowledge and understanding are finite. We are human and always partially blind. This realization causes me to have an amazing amount of gratitude for the ability to rely on and trust in the one who does know it all. God knows that whole story, each detail. I am grateful for the Holy Spirit and God's word that guides us as we spend time with the knower of all.

"For through him God created everything in the heavenly realms and on earth. He made the things we can see and the things we can't see—such as thrones, kingdoms, rulers, and authorities in the unseen world. Everything was created through him and for him. He existed before anything else, and he holds all creation together" (Colossians 1:16–17).

PERRY

*I*N THE FIRST YEARS OF our marriage, Truitt and I spent a lot of time with our fellow newlywed friends, Jim and Cindi. Each of our small apartments were lovingly decorated with our harvest gold and avocado green wedding gifts, and everything about life seemed bright and new. In those days before children, I carefully polished my beloved house plants each week with a mixture of milk and water, and we adopted a dog as soon as we moved into a tiny rent house. Cindi, who probably polished her house plants as well, adopted a parakeet named Perry.

We loved our dog and our bird like they were our babies. My weary coworkers must have been so tired of looking at all the polaroid dog pictures that I crammed into their faces, but they never complained. I believe that Cindi beat me, though, on her maternal feelings toward her pet. Perry had the finest cage and lots of toys. She spoke to him throughout the day and tended to him constantly. She worried so much about Perry that when we went out in the evening as couples, we had to run by her in-law's house to drop off Perry. He could *not* stay alone without a babysitter. No way! Truitt and I loved Perry too. I guess we felt kind of like his godparents and bought him a nice dollhouse toilet for his cage. Funny enough, he never got the hang of it.

We loved our pets, but after a short while, Jim and Cindi had a real live baby boy named Eric. I remember sitting in his nursery with Cindi and marveling at him. The pets and the plants were nice, but this was the real thing! The joy and beauty did not compare.

Just as Cindi and I longed to be moms and found some temporary substitutions, we believers are looking for the beauty of heaven. We have a lot of things that we enjoy, but they are temporary fill-ins for the incomparable wonders of heaven. Our earthly pleasures are not complete, as they are flanked on every side by stress or sorrows. Thank you, God, for giving us enjoyment on earth and for the light of your presence that illuminates our way. Thank you most of all for the real thing that is coming—beauty and joy that cannot compare!

> "No eye has seen, no ear has heard, and no mind has imagined what God has prepared for those who love him" (1 Corinthians 2:9b).

CAT?

*W*HEN WE FIRST BECAME GRANDPARENTS, we developed a plan to take each grandchild on a trip with us when he or she turned ten. Arden missed the trip during her tenth year because of the COVID-19 pandemic. Because of this, we were extra determined to make sure that she had a trip with us the next year. My mom was living with us at the time, but we found a great respite care facility for her and headed to New Mexico for a week of fun. The time with our granddaughter was precious.

However, when we returned home, we discovered that my mother's cat was missing. Our cat, D.C., and my mom's cat, Mr. Hobbs, were being cared for by a loving neighbor, but Mr. Hobbs had run away. I had one day to find Hobbs before we picked up my mother from respite care. I placed ads in all the neighborhood social media groups, scoured the area, and prayed. No Mr. Hobbs.

My stomach was in knots as I went to pick up my mom. I had checked on her during the week, and the director had given me glowing reports about her ability to navigate the temporary change despite her Alzheimer's. I knew that my mom was fine, but I was sick about having to tell her about Mr. Hobbs. I felt that I had let her down. So, after our initial joyful reunion and lots of hugs, I told my mom that I had some hard news for her.

"What is it?" she asked with a frown.

"Mom," I said, "I hate to tell you this, but your cat is missing."

"Oh," Mom said. "I have a cat?"

Alzheimer's is a horrendous disease, but you must admit, it can have its perks! What a relief.

Going to my mom to tell her that news was very hard, but after one second of hearing about Hobbs, the disappointment was forgotten. Going to God with our failures and weaknesses is even harder. When we are disappointed in ourselves, we expect God to be disappointed as well. Yet, the Bible tells us something amazing. As believers, our sins are covered by Jesus's blood and forgotten. Past. Present. Future. All our sins are forgotten. When we confess to Him, the confession draws us nearer to our Father and strengthens us to live more righteously. Yet, the confession is not an atonement. The atonement was accomplished by Christ and completed in us when we accepted Him as Savior.

What a relief!

> "And I will forgive their wickedness, and I will never again remember their sins" (Hebrews 8:12–13).

VISITATION

*T*HE IDEA SEEMS LAUGHABLE NOW, but when Truitt and I were growing up, many churches gave out reward pins for perfect attendance. Hugo Fleak (name changed to protect the wonderful) had a chain of attendance pins that hung down his coat and swayed cheerfully in the breeze as he made his way into the building each Sunday. Yet, if you knew Hugo, you understood right away that he didn't wear the pins out of pride. He wore them because he was earnest. He wanted to do what was right and good.

Hugo's earnestness also compelled him to participate in church visitations each Tuesday evening. This idea involved church members pairing up and going door-to-door, inviting folks to church. Hugo was passionate about this ministry! One evening, though, many years ago, Hugo might have been just a little too passionate. Carrie, a friend of ours and a fellow high schooler, was paired with Hugo for the great door-to-door adventure. They made a few visits and then knocked on one more door. A giant man, his face reddened in anger, quickly appeared and glared down at Hugo and Carrie.

"I've told you and told you," the man bellowed, "not to bother me during my favorite Tuesday night TV program! Why can't you listen? I'm giving you just one more chance …"

"And I'm taking it!" cried Carrie as he ran. I'm pretty sure that Carrie never "visited" again.

Christ pursues us. He also asks us to pursue others. Because of Jesus's words to us in Matthew 28:16–20, known as the Great Commission, I cannot help but believe that spreading the good news of Christ is the greatest of all tasks. Nothing compares. Poor Hugo certainly did not have wisdom and finesse when it came to visitation, but he cared about the gospel, and he cared about his neighbors. I think that most of us, including myself, need just a little bit more of that kind of passion and boldness.

I remember the story of Hugo and the mad TV watcher, and truthfully, I have to admit that sometimes Hugo was the object our jokes. But time has given me a different perspective. I am not sure that I would ever want to see a list of the people who Hugo led to Christ compared to the same type of list compiled of my gospel sharing successes. We don't have to be perfect. But we must care. We must be earnest.

> "Jesus came and told his disciples, 'I have been given all authority in heaven and on earth. Therefore, go and make disciples of all the nations, baptizing them in the name of the Father and the Son and the Holy Spirit. Teach these new disciples to obey all the commands I have given you. And be sure of this: I am with you always, even to the end of the age'" (Matthew 28:18–20).

SMILING MIGHTY JESUS

ONE DAY, OUR FRIEND DEBBIE stepped into a hospital room to begin therapy on an elderly woman. The woman was very ill, so Debbie was surprised to see a giant smile on the woman's lovely face. *She is beautiful*, Debbie, thought. *What a smile!*

"What gives you that big smile today?" Debbie asked.

"Oh," the woman answered in a resonate intonation, "I've got the Smiling Mighty Jesus!"

"You do?" Debbie asked.

"Yes, ma'am! They came in here this morning and told me. 'Girl, you got the smiling mighty Jesus!' Isn't that wonderful?"

Curious, Debbie checked her chart. Evidently, the doctor had informed the woman earlier in the day that she had spinal meningitis.

"Yes," Debbie said, now smiling herself. "That is wonderful!"

The woman was confused about her disease and probably most everything else, but she sure wasn't confused about the joy of the Lord. She had the smiling, mighty Jesus in her life, and she was *glad*!

You know, as believers, we too can rejoice. Jesus smiles down on each person who believes in the gospel and receives Him as Savior. When we make that most important decision, we become children of the only Father with infinite power and might. We have the smiling, mighty Jesus! Rejoice!

> "For the Lord your God is living among you. He is a mighty savior. He will take delight in you with gladness. With his love, he will calm all your fears. He will rejoice over you with joyful songs" (Zephaniah 3:17).

WIGGING OUT

*I*T IS FUN TO LOOK back across the years and recall the vast array of hairstyles that have dominated the world of fashion. I've seen long hair, short hair, long- and short-hair combos, permed hair, and ironed hair. But, not since the '60s and '70s have I seen the trend of wearing wigs. Wigs were big back then, and my mother embraced the style. She got her hair rolled and teased and sprayed each week at the beauty shop, and her wig, which was styled into the same poufy splendor, could be donned at a moment's notice if her regular hairstyle collapsed.

I, on the other hand, hated my mom's wig and everything it represented. You see, I was a very, very cool (at least in my own mind!) hippie wannabe. My friends and I wore our hair long and straight, and we turned up our teenaged noses at the very idea of hairspray. But one day when I was sixteen, my friend Janet and I spotted my mom's wig on the counter and decided to try it on. After all, we reasoned, when you become a mom, you are required to wear your hair in this grown-up teased-and-sprayed style. We had better prepare ourselves.

Because we had never seen moms with long straight hair, we determined that keeping our youthful style was simply not an option for us as we aged. We took turns trying on the wig and screaming, "I look horrible!" Not once did we consider the fact that we did not have to conform to this style when we became full-fledged adults.

Looking back, I am astounded at our shortsightedness. We assumed the worst. We thought that a weekly set-and-teased-up style was our destiny. But when you think about it, I guess our fear was not surprising. Don't we all tend to accept certain destinies? Marriages are destined to become dull. Kids are destined to bring us grief. Our later years in life are destined to be full of sadness and decline.

Of course, life does bring us hardships. But as believers, we have hope and help and a heavenly Father who cares and hears us when we pray. He carries us through the dark times and sometimes supernaturally delivers us from our difficult situations. When he does not supernaturally intervene, He gives us the warmth and strength of His amazing presence.

MELINDA ROGERS

With our eyes fixed firmly on God, we can stay away from the pattern of accepting doomsday destinies. Look up. Put away dread. Your destiny is in His hands.

> "'For I know the plans I have for you,' says the LORD. 'They are plans for good and not for disaster, to give you a future and a hope'" (Jeremiah 29:11).

HOT

HOW FUN, I THOUGHT AS I drove to the snow cone stand after work to meet Emily and the boys. *We can sit outside with our sweet treats and have a great visit.* However, after a few minutes at the unshaded picnic table with our dripping snow cones, we decided to seek shelter from the blazing Texas heat.

"Let's sit in my car," I said. "I will turn on the AC. It's a matter of survival!"

Emily sat in the front with me, and the boys enjoyed their snow cones from the back, bouncing up and down and chatting away. After the visit was over and everyone said their goodbyes, I pulled my car into the street and began the long drive home.

Wait a minute, I thought after a few minutes of driving. *Something is not right.*

I had my car's air conditioner on full-blast, but I was still warm. Very warm. I called Truitt in dismay and complained. "We just bought this car, and the air conditioner is already out! I'm driving and burning up!"

"Don't worry," he told me, "I will look at it when you get home." He did. He laughed. I laughed.

The air conditioner worked just fine. The boys had simply messed with the back seat controls and turned the back heater on full blast. My drive home had been miserable because I was believing a lie. I thought that we would have to spend a lot of money on a new air conditioner. I thought that I would have to be without my car for a few days. I thought and thought, but all my thoughts were erroneous. My erroneous thoughts made me recall a book I read many years ago called *The Lies We Believe* by Dr. Chris Thurman. The front jacket of the book lists the common lies that many believers take in as truth: "I must have everyone's love and approval." "My unhappiness is somebody else's fault," "I am only as good as what I do." "Life should be fair." "If our marriage takes such hard work, we must not be right for each other." "Depression, anger and anxiety are signs on a weak faith in God."

Do any of those lies sound familiar? I have probably believed most of them at one time or another. The Bible tells us in Jeremiah 17 that the heart is deceitful above all things. Yes! It is extremely easy to listen to our erroneous hearts and believe the invasive untruths that dart into our consciouses or subconsciouses.

What are the remedies? The Bible is one, of course. The Bible is true and right and good. It dispels lies. It gives strength and hope. Prayer also helps us find truth. Many times, I bow a head full of lies and raise up a head full of truth. Fellowship is also vital. Sharing our thoughts with a fellow believer can help reveal what is truth and what is not. Truth cools us down and gives us rest. Seek truth.

> "Stand your ground, putting on the belt of truth and the body armor of God's righteousness" (Ephesians 6:14).

FAMILY HISTORY

I SAT ON MY BED HOLDING a large brown envelope. I held it at arm's length in a state of stunned disbelief. *I have no idea what to do with this,* I thought. *I do not want it. I do not want my kids to have it.* The envelope held the details of my mother's family history that had been compiled by my aunt. She had been promising to send it for quite some time, and I naturally dug into the documents as soon as the package arrived. I was prepared for some darkness to my family story, but I was not prepared for the details of what I read that day. I do not even want to write about what I read about. Bleh! It was bad.

"I think I will just throw this package in the trash," I told Truitt when he arrived home.

"No way," he said. "You can't do that. Your family story is interesting!" *Interesting like a soap opera,* I thought. The what-to-do-with-the-package dilemma was resolved when I spoke to my brother, who told me that he would take it. But the problem of my sadness was not resolved. My lineage was not glorious. My lineage was rough and dark and ugly.

Then I heard a sermon. The pastor said something that I had never heard before. He spoke about Jesus's lineage. He said that the scripture of Jesus's family history that we so distractedly skim over when we read the Bible tells us a lot. Jesus had several famous sinners in his lineage, including Rahab, Ahaz, Judah, Joash, and more! Jesus, our own Savior who was without sin, came from a line of sinners. The picture was so beautiful! The history of darkness and evil was overcome by Jesus, the light. Dark history does not matter when Jesus makes all things new in the life of a believer. What a relief!

"This means that anyone who belongs to Christ has become a new person. The old life is gone, a new life has begun" (2 Corinthians 5:17).

JUST LIKE HAWAII

*A*FTER THEIR ORIGINAL POST-CHRISTMAS TRIP was scrapped due to COVID, Emily and Christopher decided to take the boys to a small camping site on a lake in South Texas. The weather was unseasonably warm, and the family found it great to be outside. However, it was winter, and it was Texas. While the lake and the sunsets were stunning in their rugged Texas way, the trees and fields were barren of leaves and flowers. This did not stop six-year-old Adrian's sense of awe and wonder.

"This looks just like Hawaii," he declared joyously. "And," he added, "When you are in Hawaii, you are supposed to stand by the water and do this." That's when the hula dance began.

Emily grabbed her phone and recorded the beautiful moves of the kindergartner whose heart was full of music. When I received the video in a text, I thought of my friends who were in Hawaii at the time. They were posting pictures on social media of scenery so lush and beautiful it almost seemed unreal. Yet, a truth that was very strong and bright caused my own heart to dance. I knew that none of those friends were any happier than the little boy on the side of a rocky lake in Texas, dancing for his family.

Oh, Lord, how I want to see the world like Adrian does. I want to dance on the rocks and not see the barrenness. I can only do this with your light, Lord. Shine in me.

> "The eye is the lamp of the body, So, if your eye is healthy, your whole body will be full of light" (Matthew 6:22).

PIONEER PHASE

AND JUST LIKE THAT THE pioneer phase was over. For several of her elementary school years, Arden lived and breathed pioneer history. We made every craft in the pioneer girls' craft book and, on multiple occasions, much to Huston's delight, made braided homemade bread. Every time she and Huston came over to spend the night, she headed straight to the grandkids' bedroom to set up her pioneer "home." The bunkbeds were rustic, and Truitt provided a basket of items left over from his mountain-man reenactments days, so Arden was in pioneer heaven. She filled the tin bowls with beans, set a small table with bone-handled forks and spatterware bowls, and lived out countless pioneer dramas that sprang from her vivid imagination.

In her early pioneer years, she would dress in costume and allow me or Truitt to be part of her story. She would not, however, allow us to do any of the script writing. The stories that we acted out were hers and hers alone. As grandparents usually do, we happily complied and enjoyed the sweet moments with our adorable pioneer. Then there was a slight shift. Arden no longer wore costumes, but she still acted out the dramas. Unlike the early years, however, Arden preferred to be alone. She allowed us in the room if we wanted, but she was happier in her own pioneer world. Our hearts hummed as we overheard her imaginative play, and we enjoyed those sweet, sweet days.

Then suddenly, Arden no longer played pioneer. When she visited, she headed straight to the grandkids' bedroom with a book. I moved the pioneer table to another room and purchased some teen floor chairs and a lamp. Our little western settler was now pioneering the teen years. The pioneer phase was over. This was a loss. Like her brother, Huston, before her, Arden was becoming a young adult, and it hurt. But history had taught me something good: Our children grow and change, and although these changes can be painful, they can also bring new facets and depths to our relationships. We come to enjoy our children in rich new ways. We enjoy our adult children immensely. When I read a good book, I want to discuss it with Clarke. When I am in need of a good chat, I know that I can call Emily.

Life is nothing but change upon change. Ecclesiastes 3:1 tells us that "there is a time for everything, and a season for every activity under the heavens." We do, indeed, go through season after season as we travel through life. But even as we and those who we love change, Hebrews 13:8 assures us that "Jesus Christ is the same yesterday and today and forever."

Our Savior and Father, who does not change, will hold our hands and hold us up as we travel through the seasons of life. Look back and remember how He has helped you navigate changes in the past. Look forward and know that the best is yet to come!

> "The way of the righteous is like the first gleam of dawn, which shines ever brighter until the full light of day" (Proverbs 4:18).

BURIED

RUITT COLLECTS OLD MAGAZINES. THEY remind us that there is "nothing new under the sun" when it comes to human problems and the old pictures and ads make us smile. Magazine collecting also makes strolling the flea markets and antique stores extra fun. Truitt never knows what paper treasure might be lurking in the very next stall.

One day, many years ago, Truitt did, indeed, find a flea market treasure, although he didn't know it at the time. He paid the usual $10.00 for a *Life* magazine with a picture of baseball great Ted Williams on the cover and was content with his find. However, a few days later, we took Clarke to a baseball card shop and were stunned. There on the wall was the very same Ted Williams magazine for sale for $300.00! We rushed home to look at the magazine that we had bought for such an incredible bargain. It was nowhere to be found. Nowhere. After much looking and reenacting and debating, we decided that the magazine must have been buried under the Sunday papers and thrown into the trash. And, yes, it must have been me that did it. Ouch. I had buried and thrown out something very valuable.

As I think about that magazine, I think of something else that we take for granted, bury, and routinely throw out: joy. We think that joy is something that will just spring up naturally when called for. We prioritize accomplishments and tasks above it. We bury it in our day-to-day worries and cares. Yet, joy is fuel for our souls' energy. We can plod onward without it, but what a dry and desolate journey that will be. Joy is a light in our spirits that must be prized and prayed for.

Paul fervently prayed for joy for the people of the church when he wrote in Romans 15:13, "May the God of hope fill you with all joy and peace as you trust in Him, so that you may overflow with hope by the power of the Holy Spirit." Pray for joy. As believers in Jesus Christ, we are blessed with an unstoppable light and hope. Don't bury these special gifts; pray that they will spring up into a roaring fire of joy. Pray for joy that

MELINDA ROGERS

fuels you forward to serve Him in ways that your former "joy-burying" self never thought possible!

> "Come everyone! Clap your hands! Shout to God with joyful praise!" (Psalm 47:1).

TEETH

HEN I WAS FIVE, I developed a case of scarlet fever. My doctor prescribed a new drug that cured my illness but that turned my incoming adult teeth gray. I sometimes wonder if that same drug sent a sneaky message to my incoming teeth that destroyed their sense of direction. I wonder this because, when my giant new adult teeth came in, they forgot to grow downward like good, obedient, rule-following teeth. They grew sideways instead, aiming toward my lips, obviously hoping to set the world's record in champion buck-toothery.

Since I was unable to eat a sandwich and looked rather unusual, my parents rushed me to an orthodontist for braces. Before the braces, I was referred to a speech therapist. Evidently, the dental folks did not believe that my teeth had simply failed to grow in the right direction. They blamed me.

"She does not know what to do with her tongue. She is a tongue thruster. She must go to tongue school." Well, they didn't say it just like that, but that was the basic gist of their proclamation. I ended up in speech therapy doing tongue exercises with chiclet gum and spending a lot of time studying a plastic head with a plastic mouth. Then came the years of braces and head gears and retainers. Finally, in junior high, my braces came off, and my teeth were straight. But instead of proclaiming how beautiful my teeth looked, my fellow preteen friends, seeing my unveiled teeth for the first time, said, "Huh. Why are your teeth gray?"

Fortunately, I met Truitt a few years later, and he proclaimed to love my gray teeth. I didn't really believe him, but I appreciated his sentiment. I do know that my gray teeth did not slow down his love for me and, in the course of time, we got married. White gown. Gray teeth. But it worked!

As if my teeth had not caused me enough humiliation, my first dentist appointment after our wedding brought quite a bit more. After examining my teeth, the dentist was shocked. I had ten cavities. I don't know why. I think I have had only two cavities in the years since then. It was a strange turn of events. But hearing the report of ten cavities was nothing compared to what happened next.

The hygienist led me into a little room with a TV screen. "Here you go," she said. "The dentist wants you to watch this." Yes, you probably guessed it, I had to sit in the little room and watch a children's video on how to brush your teeth. Although I have never had trouble with cavities since then, my dental humiliation has continued. My nemesis is tartar.

The following is a conversation I once had with a dental hygienist and is typical of my experience.

"Are you flossing each day?" "Yes," I reply proudly.

"Are you sure?" she asks with disdain. "You have so much buildup."

This is the conversation Truitt almost always has with the dental hygienist. "Are you flossing?"

"No."

"Hmm. Interesting. Your teeth look fantastic. Great job!"

I don't know why this man with white teeth and praise upon praise from hygienists stays with his dentally challenged wife, but he does. And although my teeth have brought me a lot of embarrassment over the years, I am grateful for them. My teeth allow me to eat, talk, and sing. They are the teeth that God allowed in my life, and I am thankful.

Some people have perfect teeth. Some don't. Some people can paint beautiful pictures. Some can't. Some people can solve intricate math problems. Some cannot. Some people are born to be thin. Some are not. God made us. He loves us. He knows what helps us grow and shifts our focus from selfish pride to selfless gratitude for what really matters. Thank you, God!

> "For I want you to understand what really matters, so that you may live pure and blameless lives until the day of Christ's return" (Philippians 1:10, NLT).

GIFT GRIEF

I WAS SURPRISED ONE DAY WHEN a close friend with a great spouse complained about gift shopping for her husband. "He never, ever likes anything I buy for him. He doesn't say that, of course, but it is obvious. He never wears or uses anything that anyone gives him."

I assured her that I understood what that feels like. My dad was the same. My mom tried for years to find something that he would enjoy. She bought clothes, jewelry, shoes, a fishing lease, books, and everything else she could think of. Nothing pleased him. When I grew into adulthood, I was sure that I could find something he would enjoy. I once even wrote a poem about him and had it framed. The poem did nothing for him. Nothing ever did. I don't know why.

As my father aged and became less socially aware, he gave up even trying to pretend that he liked his gifts. One memorable Christmas, he opened the gift that we had selected and carefully wrapped for him. The first words out of his mouth were not words of thanks but, "Did you keep the receipt?"

Of course, that phrase is now a family joke. Truitt and I often tease each other with those humorously discourteous words when we open gifts from each other. I think of my dad and his inability to enjoy gifts when I think about satisfaction. I suspect that my dad wanted to enjoy the presents that were given to him, but for reasons unknown, he didn't have the capacity to appreciate them. I believe that on some level, we all struggle with being satisfied. We get married and then find fault with our spouses. We buy a house and then quickly become dissatisfied with the money and work that it requires. We pray for children, but then when they are born, we pray for a few minutes of alone time and peace. We complain about our jobs, our weight, our relatives. Dissatisfaction runs rampant in the human heart and mind. Dissatisfaction kills joy, and a joyless life has very little capacity for worshiping and serving God. Dissatisfaction depletes our fuel and leaves us weak.

How do we learn to enjoy the gifts that God has given us? We thank Him daily for the blessings He has given to us. Corrie Ten Boom told a story in her book *The Hiding Place* about her sister, Betsie. Corrie could not understand how Betsie could possibly thank God for the fleas and lice that lived with them in their prison camp beds, but she did. Later, though, she and Betsie discovered that the guards refused to enter their dorm because of these creeping, crawling varmints. This freedom from watching eyes allowed these sisters and the other prisoners to hold Bible studies without fear and interruption.

When dissatisfaction raises its ugly head, drop to your knees and thank God for the gifts that He has given. He knows what you need and when you need it. Spend time in His word and let the spirit shift your priorities as you read. And whatever you do, never ask, "Did you keep the receipt?" when you open a present.

> "Let all that I am praise the LORD; with my whole heart, I will praise his holy name. Let all that I am praise the Lord; may I never forget the good things he does for me. He forgives all my sins and heals all my diseases. He redeems me from death and crowns me with love and tender mercies. He fills my life with good things. My youth is renewed like the eagle's!" (Psalm 103:1–5).

YOU SO FUNNY

*W*HEN HUSTON WAS A BABY, he thought his name was You. It makes perfect sense when you think about. All day long, he heard phrases like "You are so cute." "You need to eat your banana." "You did it!" He entertained his parents and grandparents greatly as he referred to himself as You in his first simple sentences. One of my favorite memories of Huston's early speech happened when I discovered him in our bedroom with big white dots of moisturizer all over his face.

He looked up at me with a big grin and said, "You so funny. Just like Mimi!" I didn't take a picture, but the scene is imprinted in my heart forever. He had watched me very carefully as I had applied my moisturizer earlier that day and had clearly thought that the dots were fascinating.

From an early age, our kids and grandkids are watching us. Even in the teen years when they seem to have their backs to our faces, at least metaphorically, they are watching. And others in our lives are watching as well. Nieces, nephews. Friends. Coworkers. Neighbors.

Am I trying to make you paranoid and send you to the window to lower the shade? No. Can any Christian always live a perfect life? A big, giant, colossal *no*! I am simply considering our roles as believers in Christ. How do others see us handling stress? With anger or with grace? How do others see us handling heartache? With desolation or with hope? How do others see us as we relate to the people around us? With self-importance or with humility?

Are we causing unbelievers to want to know the source of our joy? Are we encouraging fellow believers to grow in the Lord? None of us can handle everything perfectly. But we can't give up. Let's keep close to the Lord and follow his lead so that we can encourage others to love him more.

"Let us think of ways to motivate one another to acts of love and good works" (Hebrews 10:24).

MELINDA ROGERS

THE WORST

*T*HERE I WAS, RIGHT ON the first page of the knitting teacher's Facebook posts. If you looked closely, you could see that I was smiling and holding a yellow knitted blanket that was folded up in a tight ball. Emily, right next to me in the picture, was holding up a beautiful blue-and-white-striped blanket that you can see from its beautiful top to its well-knitted bottom. In fact, if you were observant, you would have seen that all twenty-four knitting students displayed in the posts are holding up lovely, completed blankets in an array of colors and styles. Except, that is, for me.

I am knitting challenged. That's why my blanket is tightly folded in the photo. Halfway through the class, I realized that I had failed to understand the end-of-row instructions and that the sides of my blanket were, shall we say, not perfect. I quickly stuffed my project in my bag and promised the teacher that I would start over and finish the blanket at home. And guess what? I did.

It is not fun to be the worst one, the one who is last and must start over. Yet, I have been the worst at bowling. I have been the worst at running. I have been the worst at line dancing. I have even been the worst at growing the easy-to-grow, ever-multiplying zucchini squash. Last year, I had easy-to-grow, ever-multiplying zucchini flowers, but not one squash. What did I do wrong?

Failure. The very word brings us down. But we all have failures. Some big, some small. We all have times when we are the worst. It is so very easy to measure our value by what we can do and by what we accomplish. Yet, God looks at the heart. Sometimes we have the worst abilities. Sometimes we have the worst attitudes. Sometimes we have the worst self-control. Sometimes we make the worst mistakes. When we are the weakest, we need to remember who is the strongest.

One of the best-loved children's songs, "Jesus Loves Me," says it well. "I am weak, but you are strong." The songs most basic truth should also ring in our ears when we are feeling like failures. "Yes, Jesus loves me. Yes, Jesus loves me. Yes, Jesus loves me. That Bible tells me so." We have great value in the eyes of the one who created us and rules over all of creation! I am weak. He is strong. He loves me. That love trumps all and his strength replaces our weakness.

> **"Each time he said, 'My grace is all you need. My power works best in** weakness.' So now I am glad to boast about my weaknesses, so that the power of Christ can work through me. That's why I take pleasure in my weaknesses, and in the insults, hardships, persecutions, and troubles that I suffer for Christ. For when I am weak, then I am strong" (2 Corinthians 12:9–10).

ALIENS

THE FATHER-SON MOVIE NIGHT WAS a great success. Truitt and twelve-year-old Clarke had the house to themselves and decided to watch *Aliens*, a fascinating, yet scary film. When Emily and I came home, we heard lots of stories about the movie, and everyone went to bed in high spirits.

We were just drifting off to sleep when Truitt woke to the sound of breathing on his side of the bed. He slowly opened his eyes and saw Clarke rocking back and forth on his feet in quiet but undisguised distress. Before Clarke could even open his mouth, Truitt realized that the scary scenes from the movie had most likely been playing in his son's mind in terrible repetition. He also realized that admitting to being scared is not something that twelve-year-old boys enjoy.

Before Truitt could even speak, Clarke saw his dad's opened eyes and took the lead. "Hey," he said in an upbeat tone, "Want to watch some Dick Van Dyke?"

"Sure!" Truitt said, as if getting out of bed to watch our family's favorite sitcom was an everyday occurrence.

I was awake by then, and my heart was warmed by the sounds of their laughter and the knowledge that my husband had seen our son's distress and had lovingly come to his rescue. My husband is a great man and is a wonderful father. Yet, I know without a doubt that our heavenly Father knows more, cares more, and loves more than any earthly father could ever know, care, or love.

Sometimes I am ashamed of my fears. I do not want to approach God with my weakness. Yet, God already knows. He knows the big picture and knows every detail of my life. God cares. A loving, good father always cares for his child. God loves us and wants us to come to Him for strength and help. Our Father understands. We are weak, but He is strong.

"Then Jesus said, 'Come to me, all of you who are weary and carry heavy burdens, and I will give you rest. Take my yoke upon you. Let me teach you, because I am humble and gentle at heart, and you will find rest for your souls. For my yoke is easy to bear, and the burden I give you is light'" (Matthew 11:28–30).

BYE, DYE

Y COUSIN MARGARET SUE WAS getting married. And I, a skinny-legged fifth grader, could hardly believe my good fortune. I was to be in the "house party." And though I wasn't exactly sure what that meant, I did understand something very important. I was to wear a dress, and a very fancy one at that, that matched the theme of the wedding. My just-on-the-cusp-of-a-teenage heart rejoiced, and the shopping began full force.

My mother purchased yards of mint green taffeta that she sewed into a dress that made a delicious ruffling sound as I walked. And to make things even more exciting, a beautiful dress such as this could not be paired with my usual white- or black-patent shoes, oh no! This dress and this occasion called for shoes that were dyed to match! My twelve-year-old heart beat fast as we selected the perfect flats and left them at the shoe store to be dyed. And, as icing on the proverbial cake, we purchased sheer mint green stockings to match.

A few weeks later, we drove to Rusk for the wedding, and I emerged from our hotel room a twelve-year-old, slightly awkward vision in mint. I had my dress, my shoes, my stockings, and, oh, yes, my first-ever wedding corsage. I felt royal. I felt beautiful. I felt water. What?

I had not seen the water puddle until it was too late. I stepped out of it to see something awful. The puddle water had turned slightly green, and the toes of my shoes had turned white. Yes, with one misstep, my dyed shoes had largely returned to their original white. Of course, solid white would have been fine. But these shoes were part white, part green, and part mud. I no longer felt glamorous, especially after getting a run in my stockings before we reached the church. But I made it through. I enjoyed the wedding and did my best to serve cake onto the beautiful glass plates at the reception. I probably grew up a little that day.

My mint green dream attire had boosted my confidence, but it had failed me. I still find myself tending to trust in the fallible things as my confidence. Some days, it is my bank account, some days it is my relationships, some days it is my talents—the list can go on and on. But all these earthly things can change and fall away. When I am discouraged,

I do a heart check through prayer and often find that I am trusting in my own resources and not in the Lord. Trusting in ourselves leads to messy puddles of disappointment. Confidence in the Lord leads to hope.

> "But blessed is the one who trusts in the Lord, whose confidence is in Him" (Jeremiah 17:7).

SOUNDED LIKE A GOOD IDEA

C LARKE WAS IN THE FIRST grade when I heard Josh McDowell give a parenting talk on the radio. He gave several ideas on parenting enrichment and told a heartwarming story about kidnapping his son early from school for an afternoon of fun. *What a great idea*, I thought. *I will kidnap Clarke a little early from school today and we will go to the park and feed the ducks*. I could hardly wait for our beautiful and memorable experience.

Emily was already home from preschool, so I buckled her into the car, and off we went to pick up her brother. We walked happily into the school and discovered Clarke in the line in the hallway with his classmates. But instead of the look of joyful surprise that I had anticipated, Clarke looked at me in horror.

"What are you doing here?" he asked.

I explained to him our plan, spoke with his teacher, and we headed to the car.

"But I don't want to go to the park," Clarke complained dramatically. "I want to watch *Transformers*!"

"Well," I waivered, "I guess we don't have to go to the park."

Then Emily piped in loudly and with lots of hot tears. "But I want to go to the park! I want to feed the ducks!"

"No!" yelled Clarke. "I want to watch *Transformers*!"

The surprise turned out to be an unexpected sibling squabble. We went to the park, fed the ducks, and then rushed home so that Clarke could still watch most of his show. We had a memorable afternoon, all right, but not for the reasons I had hoped. It was memorable because an idea I had believed to be good was quite bad. Sometimes our bad ideas bring comical results like the infamous failed kidnapping-your-kid-from-school idea of 1985. Yet sometimes they are not funny at all. Sometimes we make poor business decisions, bad relationship decisions, or other unwise choices that bring us great harm.

Where do we turn when our bad choices bring us down? God. Who loves to torment us with guilt? The enemy. Who gives us hope and promises to direct our path? God. Who should listen to God and His direction and ignore the enemy? All of us fallible, humble believers.

> "My health may fail, and my spirit may grow weak, but God remains the strength of my heart, He is mine forever" (Psalm 73:26).

SCHOOL NURSE

*T*HE POOR NURSE. SHE DIDN'T have a clue. If my friends Susan, Tina, or I got tired of sitting in our high school classes and wanted to leave early for the day, we simply used our foolproof early dismissal technique. I don't know how we devised this scheme, but it worked every time we employed it. If Friend A wanted to go home, she would simply go to the nurse's office and complain of a physical ailment.

Like clockwork, the nurse would say, "OK, let me call your mother. What is your phone number?"

Friend A would give the phone number of the pay phone in the hallway. Friend B or C would be eagerly waiting to answer the hallway phone and imitate the mother of the "ailing" girl.

"Oh, yes," B or C would say, "She has not been feeling well. I will be there right away to pick her up."

The nurse would write up an official early dismissal form, and friend A was free for the day. I am happy to report that neither Susan nor Tina nor I became professional scammers. Whew! The three of us are still friends, and as we look back on this funny little scheme, we are amazed at two things. First, we are amazed at the gullibility of the nurse. Second, and more profoundly, we are amazed at our youthful lack of conviction over our cunning little ruse. We needed a giant dose of self-examination! And although I am happy to report that I am no longer running a scam, I am still in constant need of contemplating my thoughts and deeds. We live with our own self-centeredness in a world that hates truth. Consequently, even those who desire to live righteously can be blind.

When we go to God and ask Him to reveal our tangled, misguided thoughts and wrong actions, He will. When in a mindset of confession, we ask God to direct our steps and help us, He will. Let's not be scammed by the lies of this world! God will show us the way.

"Search me, O God, and know my heart; test me and know my anxious thoughts, Point our anything in me that offends, you and lead me along the path of everlasting life" (Psalm 139:23–24).

GOOD RIDDANCE!

$\mathcal{E}$ MILY CALLED ONE SATURDAY AND overheard my quick goodbye to Truitt as he stepped into his truck.

"Where is he going?" she asked. "To do some archery?"

I must have been tired because the words, "He just changed his oil and is taking the used oil to the oil recycling center at Walmart," seemed way too hard for me. Instead, I said, "He just changed his oil and is taking it to the "get rid of it" place at Walmart."

She started to chuckle, and I joined in. Soon, we were listing all the things we would like to take the "get rid of it" place. I would take the brown spots on my hands, the corrosion recently discovered on our air conditioning unit, the looming capital gains tax on the sale of a house, several deep-seated scars of pain and hurt and my ever-present fears.

This is only a partial list. I am not sure that my actual list would have an end. What about you? What would you take? Your poor health or the health of someone you love? Your job? Your complete lack of direction for your future? Don't lie. I know that some of you would like to bring in your spouse or teenagers for some major recycling. Of course, what you long for is an opportunity to see those bad, angry, or selfish attitudes recycled into kindness and peace. If only. Sadly, the "get rid of it" place does not exist at Walmart. But it does exist with our Lord—and with God only.

We can come to Him and lay down our burdens. He listens. He cares. He hears our prayers. Some unwanted things He takes away. Some, He gives us the strength and wisdom to endure. But when we come to Him and talk, our burdens are lightened, and our perspectives are made clearer. You can talk to Him about things that are deep inside. The things that hurt and gnaw and corrode. He will heal. He will direct. He is our Father. God rids of us the darkness and brings in His light.

> "Jesus spoke to the people once more and said, 'I am the light of the world. If you follow me, you won't have to walk in darkness, because you will have the light that leads to life'" (John 8:12).

SURPRISE

I WANTED TO MAKE IT TO the finish line. If I could run a mile without pausing, I would make an A in my college body building class. It was test day, and I was determined to get a good grade. Yet, my body began to weaken, and my lungs ached and failed me. *How can an eighteen-year-old who has worked all semester for this not even make it a mile*, I pondered. Yet, I couldn't.

Tests later in my life revealed that I suffer from a type of asthma, but I didn't know that at the time. I felt like a failure. I left the track before the finish line and started the long walk to my dorm. But I couldn't even walk. I sat down and watched the stars that were dancing in front of me. *Hey*, I thought, *those stars that circle people's heads in old cartoons are a real thing!* At least I now understood some of the scenes from *Popeye* and the Roadrunner cartoons. The thought made me smile.

Then it hit me. How was I ever going to make it back to my room in time to attend my other classes? I literally could not move. It was at that moment that I saw him. Truitt pulled up in his old white Chevy. That Chevy seemed like a chariot straight from heaven, and I was in awe that my boyfriend somehow knew that I needed him. As he approached, I circled my arms around my hero as the stars continued to encircle my head. What a much-needed and happy surprise! I was rescued!

I remember this surprise well, but it will never compare to the surprise that will come to all believers one day. Because we have only seen earth, we cannot imagine heaven. I suspect that when we open our eyes in heaven, we will have a surprise greater than any of us can comprehend. I suspect that we will laugh and say, "Why did I ever fear death? Why did I spend any time at all worrying about it? Nothing compares to this. Death has brought me *real* life. Wow!"

Our great rescuer, Jesus, died a terrible death as a sacrifice for us. He overcame death and rose from the grave to demonstrate the hope that we have when we believe in him and trust him as savior. Let's be thankful and look forward to the greatest surprise of all. Thank you, Jesus.

"I pray that God, the source of hope, will fill you completely with joy and peace because you trust in him. Then you will overflow with confident hope through the power of the Holy Spirit" (Romans 15:13).

Printed in the United States
by Baker & Taylor Publisher Services